Java™ Platform Performance

Java™ Platform Performance

Strategies and Tactics

Steve Wilson
Jeff Kesselman

Addison-Wesley

Boston • San Francisco • New York • Toronto • Montreal
London • Munich • Paris • Madrid
Capetown • Sydney • Tokyo • Singapore • Mexico City

The publisher offers discounts on this book when ordered in quantity for special sales. For more information, please contact:

> Pearson Education Corporate Sales Division
> One Lake Street
> Upper Saddle River, NJ 07458
> (800) 382-3419
> corpsales@pearsontechgroup.com

Library of Congress Control Number: 00-132832

Text printed on recycled and acid-free paper.

ISBN 0-201-70969-4
1 2 3 4 5 6 7 8 9 MA 03 02 01 00
First Printing, June 2000

To Katie.
—S.W.

To my parents, who taught me to write, reason, and question.
To Dr. Timothy Allen, who taught me to think in terms of systems.
To Dr. Harry Kniaz, without whom my career would not have been possible.
—J.K.

Contents

Preface

Author's Note

In 1997, I was hired as a contractor to work on the Java™ Foundation Classes (JFC) Swing toolkit (Swing). This was an ambitious endeavor—Swing was slated to become the new standard for developing Graphical User Interfaces (GUIs) with the Java programming language. Prior to the release of Swing, the only GUI toolkit available with the Java platform was the Abstract Window Toolkit (AWT), a fairly primitive GUI toolkit by 1990s standards. While AWT was hobbled by a "lowest common denominator" design, Swing was designed to be a state-of-the-art toolkit. Written entirely in the Java programming language, it offered a powerful Model-View architecture, an advanced widget set, and a revolutionary pluggable look-and-feel (PLAF) system. When JFC was released in mid-1998, it was quickly adopted by thousands of eager developers.

As with any successful new product, along with stories of success came some bitter complaints. Some developers complained about architectural and philosophical issues. Others complained about bugs or the lack of a particular feature. However, the complaints I personally found most troubling were that programs written with Swing were slow.

I convinced my manager to let me spend a week looking into Swing's performance issues, downloaded a trial copy of a profiling package, and started poking at different parts of the toolkit.

It turned out that there were several areas where performance improvements could be made relatively easily. At the end of the week, I wrote a report on my findings and sent it to the rest of the Swing engineering team. Other members of the team got caught up in the spirit of performance tuning and began doing their own analyses. Over the next few months, I spent more and more of my time working on analysis and tuning and the Swing team made numerous performance enhancements. Many of the techniques described in this book are based on the knowledge gained while we were tuning Swing.

In late 1998, we shipped a new version of Swing that was more than twice as fast for typical tasks than the previous release. However, while many developers were pleased with the improvements, we were troubled to see that we still received numerous complaints about performance. Clearly the problem was more complex than we first thought.

I joined the performance team in Sun's Java Software unit in late 1998 and worrying about performance issues became my full-time job. In an effort to better understand the performance issues we and our developers face, I spend a lot of time talking with developers who are working on serious, real-world Java technology-based systems. Developers sometimes point out areas where changes in the libraries or VM could improve the performance of their programs. Part of my group's charter is to help make sure those changes, when appropriate, make their way into the runtime environment.

When working with developers, we also often find areas where changes to their program code can improve performance. We've found that there are a number of common mistakes and misconceptions about the performance characteristics of Java technologies and even about performance tuning in general.

The goal of this book is to share what we've learned about performance tuning Java technology-based systems with a wide audience. We hope that it will prove to be a valuable reference for you.

Steve Wilson
Sun Microsystems

About This Book

The information in this book will help you write high-performance software for the Java platform. It presents both high-level strategies for incorporating performance tuning into your software development process and code-level performance tuning tactics.

The two parts of the book approach performance tuning from different perspectives, providing a holistic view of the performance tuning process.

Part I: Strategies provides a high-level overview of the performance tuning process. It focuses on general strategies that you can incorporate into the development process to improve the performance of Java technology-based systems.

Part II: Tactics focuses on specific techniques for improving performance once you've figured out where the hot spots and bottlenecks are.

The higher-level information in the Strategies part is intended for a broad audience, including software engineers, engineering managers, technical leads, and quality assurance specialists involved in the development of Java technology-based solutions. The information in the Tactics part is geared toward intermediate to advanced developers familiar with the Java programming language who are looking for concrete coding techniques they can use to speed up their software.

The Strategies chapters are best read as a single piece, but the Tactics part does not need to be read linearly—you can go directly to whatever topic interests you most.

The two appendices at the end of the book provide information about garbage collection and the HotSpot™ virtual machine (VM) and how they can impact performance.

Performance Measurements

Unless otherwise noted, all performance measurements described in this book were run on a pre-release build of the Java 2 Standard Edition (J2SE) v. 1.3 using the HotSpot Client VM on the Microsoft Windows operating system.

Specific performance results are only representative of the configuration on which they are run. Factors such as the CPU, hard disk, operating system, and Java runtime environment (JRE) can all impact performance—keep in mind that the same benchmarks run under different configurations might yield substantially different results.

Code Samples

Complete code for the snippets, sample programs, utilities, and benchmarks used in this book is available online at *http://java.sun.com/docs/books/performance/*.

Acknowledgments

We would like to thank the many people who contributed to the success of this book.

Jon Kannegaard, Larry Abrahams, and Graham Hamilton provided the initial push that started this project. We especially need to thank Larry, who provided much needed management support throughout the project.

Lisa Friendly and Tim Lindholm, editors of the Java Series, patiently guided two first-time authors through the process of making this book a reality.

Mike Hendrickson and Julie DiNicola from Addison-Wesley were immensely helpful throughout the entire process.

Deborah Adair of The Design Cage served as part editor, part graphic designer, and part writing coach. We couldn't have finished the project without her help.

Hans Muller, the technical lead for Project Swing and the foremost expert on Swing's threading model, provided the material for Chapter 11, Writing Responsive User Interfaces with Swing. He spent many nights and weekends working on this chapter so the rest of us could better understand how to use threads in Swing programs.

Alan Sommerer contributed to the outline and organization of early drafts, ensuring that key concepts were not missed.

David Wilson and Doris Chen began writing a two-day training course on performance tuning about the same time we started working on this book. We exchanged many ideas with them and believe both the course and the book benefited.

Over the past year, Agnes Jacob introduced us to many developers who had performance-related issues. These experiences were invaluable in deciding what information to include in this book.

Many people provided a tremendous amount of input to the book by reviewing early drafts or providing important technical tidbits: Eric Armstrong, Tom Ball, Clifford Crick, Mark Davidson, Joshua Engel, Peter Haggar, Howard Harkness, Cay Horstmann, Peter Kessler, Gary Little, Mike Martak, Mike McCloskey, Dave Mendenhall, Philip Milne, Srdjan Mitrovic, Bill Pataky, Nancy Schorr, and David Stoutamire.

Introduction

SINCE the Java platform was introduced in 1995 it has become highly popular among both programmers and the companies they work for because it facilitates the rapid development and deployment of new software. From the start, however, Java technology has been dogged with complaints about its speed. A recent search of the USENET group *comp.lang.java.programmer* resulted in nearly 3,000 articles that contained the words "Java" and "slow." Clearly, performance is an area of concern for many developers.

In the past few years, there have been numerous technological advances that have improved the performance of the Java platform. Just-in-time (JIT) compilers and advanced runtime systems, such as Sun's Java HotSpot Virtual Machine, have significantly improved performance. In addition, as Moore's Law dictates, computers continue to get more powerful every year. Today's average PC is an order of magnitude faster than the average PC at the time Java technology was first introduced. Despite these advances, complaints about the speed of Java technology-based programs persist.

When average hardware performance continues to get faster, and the core runtime technology continues to improve, why do so many developers continue to have performance issues? The answer turns out to be somewhat obvious. The software being developed for the Java platform today is much more complex than it was just a year or two ago. Developers are continuing to push the envelope—each time the tools improve, the scope and complexity of the applications being built with them increases. In short, the technology is fulfilling the promise that it's not just for "Dancing Duke" applets anymore.

Dancing Duke

Powerful Java technology-based enterprise systems are being deployed in situations where millions of dollars are riding on the system's success. Independent software vendors (ISVs) are replacing and trying to compete with solutions written with more traditional languages like C++.

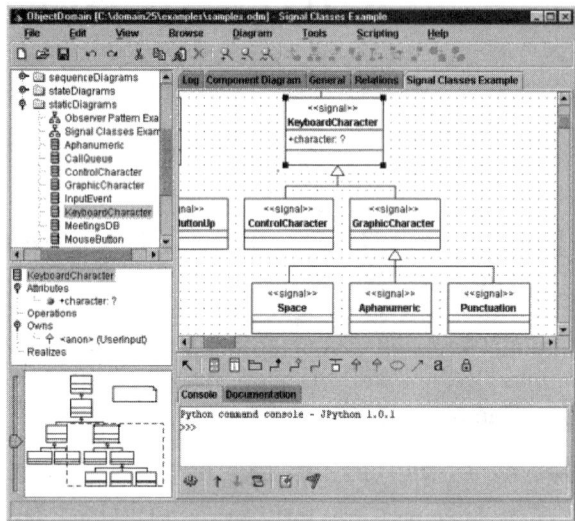

A commercial Swing-based Java application

Not only do today's Java applications go far beyond making Duke dance, these large-scale, mission-critical software solutions are more complex than anything many Java programmers have written in the past. As they continue to push the limits of the technology, developers are also being asked to solve increasingly difficult problems that push the limits of their experience.

Developing high-performance software in any language is not a trivial task. In addition to a thorough understanding of the language and libraries you're using, you need to know how to effectively fit performance tuning into your overall development process.

This book presents strategies and tactics you can use to make performance tuning a part your software development process and effectively evaluate and optimize the performance of your software.

Part I: Strategies

*Stra•te•gy (strat ə je), n., pl. -gies. 1. the style or art of planning
and directing large-scale military movements and operations.
2. a plan or method for achieving a goal.

—Random House Webster's Dictionary*

THE chapters in this part introduce strategies that you can incorporate into your development process to improve the performance of Java™ technology-based systems. Whether you're a software engineer, engineering manager, technical lead, or quality assurance specialist, this information will help you better understand how to ensure that you meet your performance goals. For specific programming tactics you can use to improve the performance of your Java technology-based programs, see Part II: Tactics (page 37).

Chapter 1, What Is Performance? (page 3)
It sounds like a simple question, but it turns out that there are several aspects of performance, each of which can be important. This chapter provides a common language for discussing performance issues and looks at the different factors that affect the performance of a Java technology-based system.

Chapter 2, The Performance Process (page 9)
Once you understand the factors that affect performance, you need to know how to fit performance tuning into your development process. This chapter reviews the typical software development cycle and shows how to make performance tuning an integral part of it.

Chapter 3, Measurement Is Everything (page 17)
It's impossible to tune your software effectively if you can't measure the effects of your changes. This chapter discusses different ways of measuring software performance and shows you how to analyze and apply the results.

CHAPTER 1

What Is Performance?

"More computing sins are committed in the name of efficiency (without necessarily achieving it) than for any other single reason—including blind stupidity."

—W. A. Wulf

BEFORE we can discuss how to improve performance, it's necessary to define what performance is. This isn't as simple as it sounds—people often mean very different things when they talk about performance. There are several aspects of performance, each of which contribute to the overall performance of an application.

Computers fascinate people with their ability to carry out tasks with blinding speed. When a computer, for whatever reason, doesn't perform a task quickly, users are disappointed. Developers often use the terms "speed" and "performance" interchangeably. However, to understand the different types of problems that can be encountered, all of the different aspects of performance must be considered:

- Computational performance
- RAM footprint
- Startup time
- Scalability
- Perceived performance

These factors lay the foundation for a better understanding of the performance landscape. Some aspects of performance are primarily applicable to client-side systems, some to server-side systems, and some to both. Understanding how each factor can contribute to the performance characteristics of a system will help you analyze the performance of your own applications.

1.1   Computational Performance

Computational performance is what most people think about first when discussing software performance. Computational performance concerns characteristics such as

- How many instructions are required to execute a statement?
- How much overhead does a particular virtual method call incur?
- Should I use a quick-sort or a bubble-sort here?

Much of the software performance literature centers on computational performance. Obviously, which algorithms you use and how you implement them are key factors in the overall performance of your software—Chapter 8 focuses on the selection and use of algorithms and data structures. It turns out, however, that this is only part of the performance picture. You need to consider factors beyond computational performance if you want to produce truly high-performance software.

1.2   RAM Footprint

The amount of memory needed to run your software can be of crucial importance to the overall performance of your system. All modern operating systems provide a virtual memory system where disk space can be used in place of physical RAM. However, even the fastest hard disk is far slower than the slowest memory module, and applications that force the operating system (OS) to page to virtual memory will generally perform poorly.

It's not uncommon for a system to perform well while under development, but perform very poorly once deployed. Because software developers typically have considerably more physical memory in their workstations than average users, a program that runs comfortably on a developer's machine might require more memory than is available when installed on a user's machine. If your software is going to be deployed on machines with limited RAM resources, you need to design your software with the target configuration in mind.

It's also important to remember that your program probably won't be the only one running on a user's machine—users typically keep two or three applications running at a time. If your program consumes all of their memory resources, your users aren't going to be very happy.

If you're like most developers, you probably have an intuitive understanding of the issues regarding memory usage, but you might not know how to accurately measure or optimize your software's RAM footprint. Two tactics chapters focus on footprint issues—Chapter 5, RAM Footprint, and Chapter 6, Controlling Class Loading.

1.3   Startup Time

For client applications, the amount of time it takes to launch a program can be critical. For example, if it takes 90 seconds to load a web page with an embedded applet, most users will never see it—they'll load a different page instead. Anyone who does wait for the applet to load is going to have a very poor impression of your program from the start that will be difficult or impossible to overcome.

Historically, systems based on Java technology have been slow to launch. If you're developing a client application, you need to watch out for this problem. Specific tactics for minimizing startup time are discussed in Chapter 6, Controlling Class Loading, and in Chapter 12, Deployment.

It's also possible for an application to run slower when it's first started than it does after it has been running for a while. More advanced Java runtime systems, such as the Java Hotspot™ virtual machine (HotSpot VM), gradually compile more and more of a program's code as they run. The speed of the application ramps up as more of the code is compiled, as shown in Figure 1-1.

In server environments, this behavior might not be a problem, but it can be a major issue for client-side systems. You should be aware that it can affect the performance of your application, particularly if it will be deployed on the client.

Appendix A provides additional information about how the HotSpot VM affects performance.

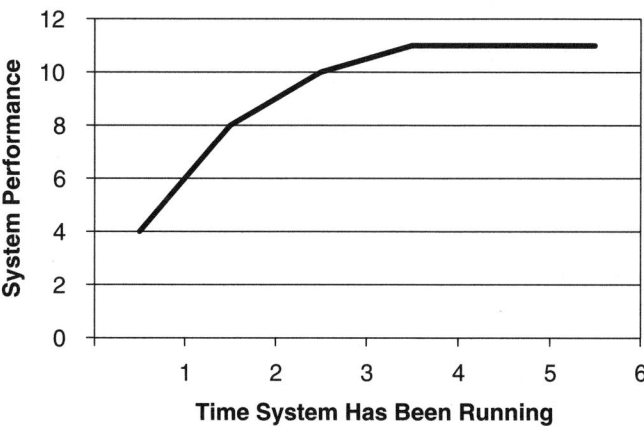

Figure 1-1   Performance improves as more code is compiled

1.4   Scalability

Scalability, the study of how systems perform under heavy loads, is an often-neglected aspect of performance. A server might perform well with 50 concurrent users, but how does it perform with 1,000? Does the performance of the server drop off gradually, or does it degrade quickly when a certain threshold is reached?

Figure 1-2 shows a theoretical system that isn't scaling well. As the number of users on the system increases, the average response time increases exponentially. This system will eventually reach a point where each user waits for an unacceptable amount of time.

In contrast, Figure 1-3 shows a system that scales in a more desirable manner. Although the average response time does increase as more users log on to the system, the response time degrades gradually.

Note that both of these systems show the same performance characteristics for small numbers of users (up to 250). It is only with larger numbers of users that the systems start to show their true characteristics. It's important to measure a system's performance under a load comparable to that which it needs to support when it's deployed.

The design decisions you make can determine whether your system will scale well or break down when heavily stressed in real-world situations. While scalability is often associated with servers, it can be just as important for client applications. For example, consider a word processor. It might work well when the user is editing a five-page letter, but how about a 200-page book? Can it handle it, or does typing slow to a crawl as the program tries to lay out the entire document each time the user presses a key?

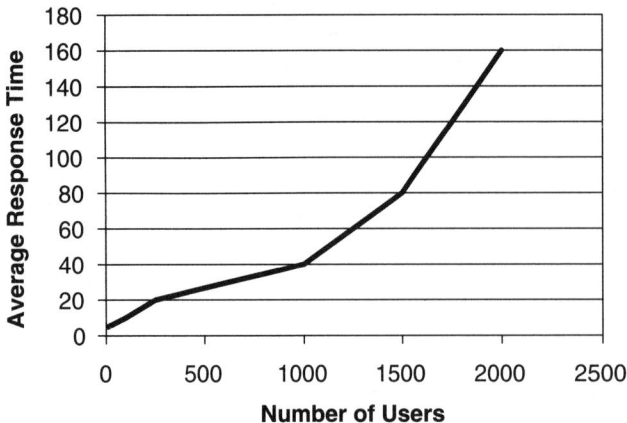

Figure 1-2   A system that doesn't scale well

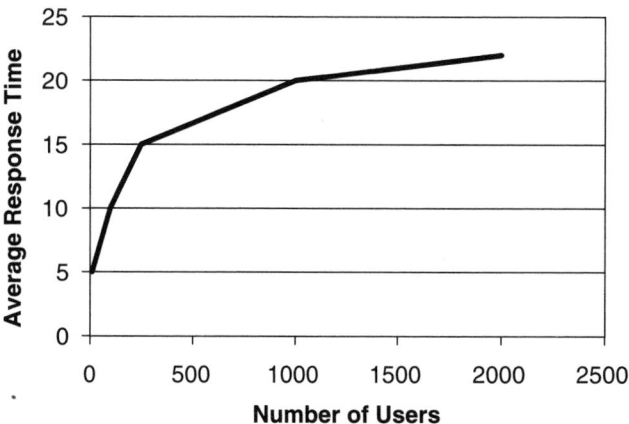

Figure 1-3 A system that scales well

It's important to be aware of potential scalability issues and design your software to accommodate its intended usage. Many techniques for ensuring that a program scales well are problem-domain specific. However, there are a number of general guidelines that can help you. Some of these are described in Section 2.1.2, Object-Oriented Design. Chapter 10, Swing Models and Renderers, contains information about developing scalable GUIs.

1.5 Perceived Performance

Perceived performance is in some ways the most important aspect of performance, especially for GUI applications. Performance is really in the eye of the beholder. Users rarely measure performance with a stopwatch—for GUI applications in particular, what's important is how fast the program *feels*, rather than how fast it really is.

It turns out that there are many ways to improve how fast an application feels to the user without actually making any of the code run faster. These range from simple things like changing the mouse cursor to a wait cursor while your application is busy, to performing complex processing with multiple background threads. It's possible to make an interface feel responsive, even when the program is waiting for data from a slow network. You'll find several examples of how to improve perceived performance in Chapter 11, Writing Responsive User Interfaces with Swing.

CHAPTER 2

The Performance Process

PRODUCING fast software is nontrivial. Performance isn't a single step in the software development process; it needs to be a part of your overall software development plan. Achieving maximum performance from your software requires continued effort throughout all phases of development, not just coding.

This chapter introduces a *performance process* that is based on standard object-oriented software development methodologies. This process includes the standard phases of a software development cycle and adds one additional phase, performance profiling.

If you're interested in learning more about object-oriented design (OOD) and the overall software development process, the resources listed in Section 2.2 are a good place to start.

2.1 Developing a Performance Process

The processes that have been developed for object-oriented software development (OOSD) are applicable to the problem of producing high-performance software. It turns out that solid analysis and design is a crucial part of the performance process. If you don't have a good analysis of the problem you're modeling, it's nearly impossible to produce a solid software design. Without a solid software design, it's nearly impossible to achieve good performance through optimizations alone.

The basic OOSD process has four main phases:

- Analysis
- Design
- Coding
- Testing

Figure 2-1 shows the steps in the performance process. These mirror the phases of the traditional OOSD model, with one addition. This new phase is *performance profiling*—determining the performance characteristics of a software system.

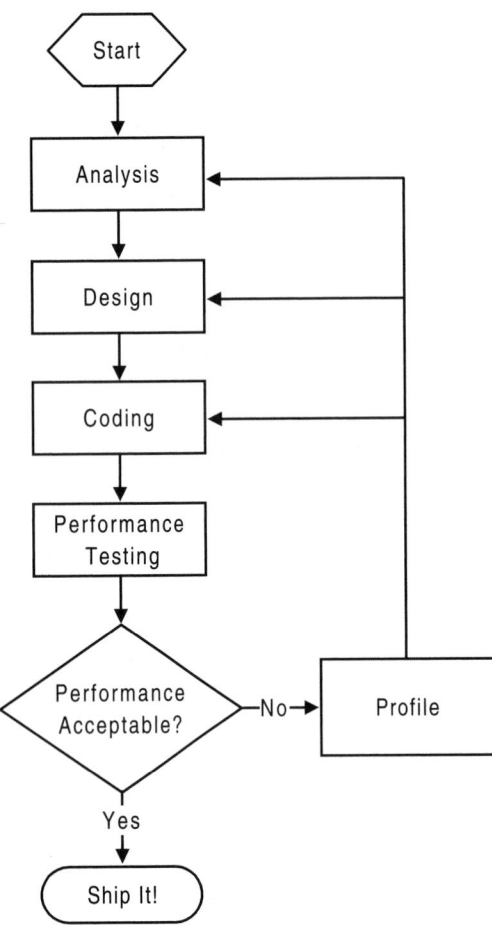

Figure 2-1   The performance process

Popular OOSD methodologies define particular tasks to be completed during each development phase. As we discuss each phase, we'll introduce some additional performance-related tasks that are critical to producing high-performance software. These complement, rather than replace, those required by the OOSD methodologies.

2.1.1   Analysis

Analysis is the first stage of the development process. It is also the first step in producing high-performance software. Analysis is central to the performance tuning process. During this phase of the development process, you shouldn't worry about low-level issues like language, syntax, classes, methods, or data structures.

Different methodologies specify different deliverables for the analysis phase. One of these is usually a software requirements specification (SRS). The SRS specifies exactly what your software is supposed to do. It generally includes a high-level analysis of the problem domain and a set of scenarios that illustrate key functionality. This information is required input to the design phase of the project.

From a performance perspective, there are some key pieces of information that need to be included in the SRS. One key item that should be included in your SRS is a set of *use cases*. Use cases are descriptions of the sequence of events and actions that occur when a user interacts with the system. They are used to describe the outwardly visible requirements of a system.[1] These descriptions can be textual, or might include diagrams. Use cases are an important step in defining the conceptual model of your system, and they are also crucial for creating testing plans and documentation. The major reason to be interested in them from a performance perspective, however, is *benchmarking*. In general, use cases can make an excellent way to determine what types of benchmarks you should create to measure the performance of your system. By basing your benchmarks on use cases, you can better ensure that your benchmarks are representative of the real-world use of your system. See Chapter 3, Measurement Is Everything, for more information about benchmarking.

In addition to the information about what the software is going to do, the SRS should specify planned limitations—what your product definitely will *not* do. What parts of the problem domain will the product not address? This information is very important—a product cannot be all things to all people. Systems that try to do everything generally fail. Well-defined boundaries on your software's scope can open up big optimization opportunities during the design and coding phases.

The SRS must also go beyond just software requirements; it needs to include system and performance requirements. System requirements include information such as:

- Minimum hardware configuration (RAM, CPU)
- Target hardware configuration (RAM, CPU)
- Target network connection speed (dial-up, 10-baseT, gigabit)

You'll also want to know whether other software is likely to be running at the same time and anything else that is peculiar to your target environment. The more information you have about your target environment, the better.

---

1. For more information about use cases, see Geri Schneider and Jason Winters, *Applying Use Cases: A Practical Guide*, p. 1. Addison-Wesley, 1998.

Once you have your basic system requirements you can define specific performance requirements. Performance requirements are the most useful when they are quantifiable. For example:

- The server should provide an average response time of two seconds or less with 100 concurrent users.
- The client program should launch in less than 15 seconds on the target hardware configuration.
- The video conferencing feature should support 24 frames per second on the minimum hardware configuration with a 10-baseT Ethernet connection.

It's not always possible to quantify all of an application's performance requirements, especially for user interface code. If a goal can't be effectively quantified, qualitative requirements are much better than no requirement at all. For example:

- The client portion of the system should provide acceptable performance when running on the minimum system configuration concurrently with Netscape Navigator 4.5.
- Scrolling should be smooth on the target configuration.

Too often, projects move from analysis, to design, to coding, and on to beta testing before the engineering team knows what the performance requirements are. The team might have the system working well in the lab on a 500MHz machine, only to find that the target customer will be using a 200MHz machine. Before you start, engineering, management, marketing, and ideally your customers should reach a consensus about the performance requirements for your system. If you don't, how will you know when your product is fast enough?

2.1.2   Object-Oriented Design

Object-oriented design plays a major role in the performance process. While there are many factors that contribute to a good design, and all of them are important, there is one concept that is especially critical to creating high-performance systems. This concept is called *encapsulation*. In his book *Applying UML Patterns*, Craig Larman defines encapsulation as "a mechanism used to hide the data, internal structure and implementation details of an object. All interaction with an object is through a public interface of operations."[2]

Encapsulation encourages you to isolate the internal structure of your objects from the rest of your program. Generally, encapsulation is discussed in the context

---

2. Craig Larman, *Applying UML Patterns: An Introduction to Object-Oriented Analysis and Design*, p. 499. Prentice Hall, 1998.

of improved software maintenance—not improved performance. In fact, there is a general perception among some programmers that encapsulation hurts performance by requiring greater data indirection and more method calls. While it is true that the increased levels of indirection lead to some slowdowns when compared to theoretical maximum performance levels, encapsulation is essential in large, scalable, high-performance systems.

Making encapsulation part of your design from the start enables you to:

- Quickly evaluate different algorithms and data structures to see which is most efficient
- Easily evolve your design to accommodate new or changed requirements

To understand how encapsulation helps in the evaluation of algorithms and data structures, let's look at an example from the Java 2 Collections Framework. The Collections Framework provides an abstraction for the concept of a List. The framework also provides several implementations of this abstraction including LinkedList and ArrayList. These are all discussed in greater detail in Chapter 8, Algorithms and Data Structures, but for now all you need to know is that these two classes have radically different performance characteristics even though they implement the same interface. Neither class is the fastest for all tasks—either can be several times faster than the other, depending on the types of operations that are performed on the List.

The increased indirection caused by the encapsulation of the list datastructures does mean that more method invocations are used to carry out operations than if the internal structures were exposed. However, this is a very small performance decrease—in typical cases, only a few percent. Contrast this with the possibility that switching from an array-based list to a linked list might result in a tenfold speedup of a critical operation in your system. If you expose the raw data structures everywhere in your program, you might have to modify hundreds of lines of code just to find out which solution is fastest. On the other hand, if you use encapsulation, you might only need to change one line of code to try the alternative solution.

A similar case is found in the Swing[3] model classes. Chapter 10, Swing Models and Renderers, shows how the use of encapsulation makes it possible for components such as JTable to scale to accommodate huge data sets.

These cases both show how the use of encapsulation inside the Java libraries is important. However, it is equally important to apply these concepts when designing your own classes.

---

3. *Swing* refers to the Java Foundation Classes (JFC) Swing packages, which provide a comprehensive set of classes for building graphical user interfaces.

Using encapsulation makes it easier to adapt to changing requirements. This is obviously important for system maintenance, but it is also critical for system performance. For example, if your initial SRS states that your system has to be able to handle up to 100 users. you might decide to store user data in flat files. If the system is so well-received during beta testing that management decides to roll it out companywide to 10,000 users, your flat-file system is probably going to become a performance bottleneck.

To eliminate the bottleneck, you need to rework the system to use an industrial-strength database to store user data. If you encapsulated your data-storage mechanism inside a set of well-designed abstract classes, moving from the flat-file structure to the database should be fairly easy. However, if the storage mechanism isn't well encapsulated and many parts of your system assume that the user data is stored in files, the rearchitecture could take a significant amount of development time.

2.1.3   Coding

Clearly, the way you write your code has an impact on how your system performs. Part II of this book shows numerous examples of how similar pieces of code can have radically different performance characteristics. However, it is important to remember that it is easy to spend a lot of time tweaking parts of your system to improve performance, even though they might not be performance-critical. Always remember that analysis, design, and profiling are at least as important as the actual coding phase of the process.

2.1.4   Testing

Quality assurance is an important part of the software development process. In this context, however, we want to focus on performance testing rather than quality testing. Performance testing is really about benchmarking. Once you have a version of your system running (even a partial system), you can begin to construct benchmarks to measure its performance. These benchmarks should be based on your performance requirements. Having a solid set of benchmarks allows you to track your progress over time and see where you are with regard to your requirements. Meeting or exceeding your performance requirements should be part of the shipping criteria for your product. Chapter 3 describes benchmarking in more detail.

2.1.5   Profiling

Many systems don't meet all of their performance requirements on the first try. Once you've determined that a performance problem exists, you need to begin profiling. Profiling determines what areas of the system are consuming the most resources. Many tools are available to help you with this process. Profilers are most useful for identifying computational performance and RAM footprint issues.

By analyzing data from a profiler, you can isolate the parts of the system that are causing your performance problems. This information can then be used to determine what changes will reap the greatest benefit. Sometimes the solution is as simple as modifying a single method, algorithm, or data structure. However, studying your system with a profiler can also reveal flaws in your OOD, and even in your original problem analysis. You need to be willing to revisit these early stages of the process. Grady Booch, a prominent object-oriented design expert, notes:

> Rigid approaches to design only lead to largely useless design products that resemble a progression of lies, behind which developers shield themselves because no one is willing to admit that poor design decisions should be changed early, rather than late.[4]

There are several good commercial profiling tools on market, and a simple free tool is included with Sun's version of the Java 2 SDK. Without a profiling tool you'll be left guessing about what parts of your system need optimization, and you risk wasting a great deal of effort optimizing code that has nothing to do with the true bottlenecks. Profiling is discussed in depth in Chapter 3.

2.2   References on Object-Oriented Design

Booch, Grady. *Object-Oriented Analysis and Design with Applications, Second Edition,* Addison-Wesley, Reading, MA, 1994.

Gamma, Erich, Richard Helm, Ralph Johnson, and John Vlissides. *Design Patterns: Elements of Reusable Object-Oriented Software*, Addison-Wesley, Reading, MA, 1995.

Goldstein, Neal, and Jeff Alger. *Developing Object-Oriented Software for the Macintosh: Analysis, Design, and Programming*, Addison-Wesley, Reading, MA, 1992.

Grand, Mark. *Patterns in Java, Volume 1*, John Wiley & Sons, New York, 1998.

---

4. Grady Booch, *Object-Oriented Analysis and Design with Applications*. Addison-Wesley, 1994.

Larman, Craig. *Applying UML and Patterns: An Introduction to Object-Oriented Analysis and Design*, Prentice Hall, Upper Saddle River, NJ, 1998.

Schneider, Geri, and Jason Winters. *Applying Use Cases: A Practical Guide*, Addison-Wesley, Reading, MA, 1998.

Key Points

- Writing high-performance software requires action during all phases of the software development lifecycle.

- Creating clear system and performance requirements is the key to evaluating the success of your project.

- Scalability is more dependent on good design decisions than optimal coding techniques.

- Performance tuning is an iterative process. Data gathered during profiling needs to be fed back into the development process.

CHAPTER 3

Measurement Is Everything

*"We should forget about small efficiencies,
say about 97% of the time: premature
optimization is the root of all evil."*

—Donald Knuth

THE level of complexity involved in modern software systems means that no human, no matter how clever, is qualified to do a proper job of performance tuning without using some basic tools. This chapter introduces tools and techniques you can use measure the performance of your software.

Two analysis techniques are crucial for evaluating performance:

- *Benchmarking*—qualitatively comparing two or more operations.

- *Profiling*—determining what areas of the system are consuming the most resources.

3.1   Benchmarking

Benchmarking is the process of comparing operations in a way that produces quantitative results. Benchmarking plays a key role in ensuring that your software performs well.

The processes being compared might be two different algorithms that produce the same results, or two different virtual machines executing exactly the same code. The key aspect of benchmarking is comparison. A single benchmark result isn't interesting—it's only useful when there is something to compare it with. Benchmarks typically measure the amount of time it takes to perform a particular task, but they can also be used to measure other variables, such as the amount of memory required.

A stopwatch can be a valuable benchmarking tool (Figure 3-1). It might seem a little silly to use a watch to help you tune high-performance software, but sometimes it's the best tool for the job. Obviously, you won't get millisecond accuracy

Figure 3-1   A primitive, but useful, benchmarking tool

with a stopwatch, but it's not always necessary to be that precise. For example, you might use a stopwatch to measure:

- How long it takes to launch an application
- How long it takes to open a large document
- How long it takes to scroll through a very large table of data
- How long it takes to execute a complex database query

Table 3-1 shows some of the trade-offs associated with stopwatch benchmarking. Overall, a stopwatch can be one of the most versatile performance-analysis tools you have at your disposal.

Although a stopwatch is a useful tool, it's clearly not appropriate for all benchmarking tasks. Another benchmarking technique that is suitable for a wide variety of situations is to add timing functionality to the code you're evaluating.

The `java.lang.System` class contains several useful static methods, including a method called `currentTimeMillis`. This method returns a `long` that contains the number of milliseconds that have elapsed since midnight, January 1, 1970. You can use this method to measure how long a particular piece of code takes to execute. Simply store the time before and after the section of code executes, then calculate the elapsed time by subtracting.

Pros	Cons
Easy	Can be inaccurate
Don't need to modify source code or use complex software tools	Hard to automate testing
Won't skew results	Subject to human error

Table 3-1   Stopwatch Benchmarking

Listing 3-1 shows a simple example that measures how long it takes to sum all of the numbers between zero and 10 million.

```
class TimeTest1 {
   public static void main(String[] args) {

      long startTime = System.currentTimeMillis();

      long total = 0;
      for (int i = 0; i < 10000000; i++) {
         total += i;
      }

      long stopTime = System.currentTimeMillis();
      long elapsedTime = stopTime - startTime;
      System.out.println(elapsedTime);
   }
}
```

Listing 3-1   Using `currentTimeMillis` to calculate execution time

This technique is essentially the same as using a stopwatch, except that the computer starts and stops the watch automatically. This technique enables you to automate benchmark tests and can increase the accuracy of your measurements.

While this type of benchmark measurement can be very useful, it can be tiresome to add this code to each operation you need to measure. You also run the risk of introducing coding errors that could affect your results.

An alternative is to encapsulate this behavior in a reusable class that emulates your stopwatch. Listing 3-2 shows an implementation of a reusable stopwatch class.

```
/**
   * A class to help benchmark code
   * It simulates a real stop watch
   */
public class Stopwatch {

   private long startTime = -1;
   private long stopTime = -1;
   private boolean running = false;

   public Stopwatch start() {
      startTime = System.currentTimeMillis();
      running = true;
      return this;
   }
   public Stopwatch stop() {
      stopTime = System.currentTimeMillis();
```

```
        running = false;
        return this;
    }
    /** returns elapsed time in milliseconds
     * if the watch has never been started then
     * return zero
     */
    public long getElapsedTime() {
        if (startTime == -1) {
            return 0;
        }
        if (running){
        return System.currentTimeMillis() - startTime;
        } else {
        return stopTime-startTime;
        }
    }

    public Stopwatch reset() {
        startTime = -1;
        stopTime = -1;
        running = false;
        return this;
    }
}
```

Listing 3-2   Reusable stopwatch class

Listing 3-3 shows how you can use this stopwatch class to measure a piece of code. Using this class is simpler than adding the timing code to each operation you want to measure and ensures that errors aren't introduced by the timing mechanism.

```
class TimeTest2 {
    public static void main(String[] args) {

        Stopwatch timer = new Stopwatch().start();

        long total = 0;
        for (int i = 0; i < 10000000; i++) {
            total += i;
        }

        timer.stop();
        System.out.println(timer.getElapsedTime());
    }
}
```

Listing 3-3   Using the Stopwatch class

3.1.1   Why Build Benchmarks?

It is important to understand why you need to write benchmarks. Most of the time when you read about benchmarks, it's in the context of comparing two different pieces of computer hardware. This CPU is faster than that CPU. This disk drive has a faster average seek time than that disk drive. The community of developers using Java technology has also created benchmarks. These benchmarks are usually designed to compare runtime implementations. Examples of these benchmarks include

- SpecJVM[1]
- VolanoMark[2]
- JMark[3]
- SciMark[4]
- CaffeineMark[5]

While benchmarks like these can be useful in evaluating implementations of the Java Runtime Environment (JRE), they can't be used to evaluate a program's performance. You need to create benchmarks that test your own code. Creating custom benchmarks enables you to

- Compare the performance of alternative solutions
- Profile the performance of your applications
- Track performance and perform trend analysis throughout the development cycle

Comparison is the most obvious use of custom benchmarks. For example, if you need to choose between two algorithms for implementing a particular function, you can create a benchmark and compare the two solutions. This is typically what benchmarks are used for. However, comparing solutions isn't the only use of benchmarks.

Using profiling tools to examine where your code is spending time is a crucial part of performance tuning, but it can be difficult to interpret the results unless you have repeatable test cases. Good benchmarks are repeatable: they do the same thing every time. This allows you to run the benchmark under the profiler and

---

1. For more information about SpecJVM, see *http://www.spec.org*.
2. For more information about VolanoMark, see *http://www.volano.com/benchmarks.html*.
3. For more information about JMark, see *http://www.zdnet.com/zdbop/jmark/jmark.html*.
4. For more information about SciMark, see *http://math.nist.gov/scimark/about.html*.
5. For more information about CaffeineMark, see *http://www.pendragon-software.com/pendragon/ cm3/index.html*.

collect data. When you make a change, you can run the benchmark under the profiler again to see how it affects the results. In some cases, this can give you better insight into your problems than simply measuring the amount of time required to execute the benchmark. Profiling is examined in more detail in Section 3.2.

The most important reason for writing benchmarks is that they enable you to track and analyze trends. As you fix bugs and add features, the performance of your software is likely to change. By running benchmarks at regular intervals, you can easily determine whether your software is getting faster or slower.

If you don't track the performance of your system as changes are made, performance can slowly degrade undetected. When the performance degradation becomes obvious, you're faced with the daunting task of figuring out what went wrong. By regularly running benchmarks on key parts of your system, you can catch performance regressions when they first occur, which makes it much easier to find and fix the problems.

Benchmarks can often be placed into one of two categories: micro-benchmarks and macro-benchmarks. Micro-benchmarks are tightly focused benchmarks that test one specific aspect of a system. Macro-benchmarks are larger, more comprehensive tests that typically exercise a larger portion of a system's functionality. While both types of benchmarks have their place, you need to be aware of their individual strengths and weaknesses.

3.1.2   Micro-Benchmarks

Micro-benchmarks can often be written in just a few lines of code and are typically very easy to describe. A micro-benchmark might perform a task such as:

- Drawing 50,000 rectangles
- Reading a 1MB file from disk
- Finding all the prime numbers between 1 and 1,000,000
- Sorting an array of 25,000 elements

Micro-benchmarks can be good for comparing different options. For example, if you want to select the optimal sorting routine for your application, you might try several different algorithms on a typical data set and choose the one that runs fastest. Or when deciding which of two classes to use for file access in your program, you might evaluate your choices with a micro-benchmark that reads in a file using both file access classes.

Micro-benchmarks are handy in a wide range of situations, but they have limitations. Micro-benchmarks often do not represent real-world behavior. A number of factors can contribute to this limitation, the two most important being Java virtual machine (JVM) warm-up and global code interactions. You need to understand these factors to write truly useful benchmarks.

Modern JVM implementations typically first execute code in interpreted mode, then switch to compilation for more time-consuming code. This means that the JVM might have to study the system for a while before it can determine the proper set of optimizations. Some JVMs can even undo previous optimizations if it turns out that they were under- or over-aggressive. This behavior leads to a phenomenon where the performance of your program starts out slow and then picks up speed as it runs. Micro-benchmarks can totally miss this behavior, leaving you with the impression that your code is very slow when it would actually run much faster in a true production environment.

For example, early versions of the HotSpot VM couldn't compile a method the first time it was executed by a program. As a result, micro-benchmarks often executed totally in interpreted mode, which made them appear much slower than they would in a production system. While this specific problem was fixed in later versions, the general issue remains.

Another major limitation of micro-benchmarks is that they often miss larger interactions and usage patterns that can have a big impact on real-world performance. For example, if you were writing a graphics library you might want to create a number of micro-benchmarks for operations such as drawing rectangles, lines, and text. You might create one micro-benchmark that draws 50,000 rectangles of different sizes and colors, one that draws 50,000 lines of varying length, and another that draws 50,000 random strings.

Once these benchmarks are in place, you could use them to measure performance progress as you tune. You might even use them for profiling. To some extent these benchmarks would be useful, but there are some serious problems with this approach. Benchmarks like these can miss key interactions that affect the performance of your application as seen by actual users. For example, complex graphic images rarely consist of 50,000 rectangles drawn in sequence; they typically consist of a combination of rectangles, lines, and text. By tuning for a small set of micro-benchmarks, you could inadvertently make optimizations that speed up the uncommon case of executing many similar operations, while slowing down the common case of mixing different types of operations.

3.1.3 Macro-Benchmarks

Although micro-benchmarks are useful in some situations, you also need to build some macro-benchmarks. True macro-benchmarks test your system as actual end users will see it. In the case of the graphics library, rather than creating yet another micro-benchmark that draws one rectangle, one line, and one piece of text and repeating the operation 50,000 times, it would be more useful to create a macro-benchmark that operates on some real-world data.

To build a meaningful macro-benchmark, you need to understand how your customers are going to use your product. For example, the graphics library might be tailored for building high-end CAD/CAM packages. A good macro-benchmark for this product would be a test module that reads a standard CAD data file format and renders the image from several different angles. Real blueprints could then be used as the test data. By creating this sort of macro-benchmark, you're much more likely to catch global interactions that affect performance.

Ideally, you want to use benchmarks that test your system in a true production environment. For example, if you're producing a web site that uses Java servlets or JavaServer Pages™ technology,[6] you should test them using the same web server software on which you'll deploy your site. Ideally, you should also simulate the typical load that your server will experience when you run your benchmarks.

The Apache Software Foundation provides a tool called `JMeter`, shown in Figure 3-2, that can help you with this type of testing. For more information, see *http://java.apache.org/jmeter/index.html.*

It's important to remember that macro-benchmarks aren't just for server-side applications. They are also important for client-side applications. For example, possible macro-benchmarks for client applications might measure

- Application start-up time

- Application RAM footprint (benchmarks aren't always measured in seconds)

- The time it takes to open and display a large document

- The time is takes to scroll through a large document

One excellent source of material for macro-benchmarks is the set of use cases developed during the analysis phase of your project (see Section 2.1.1 on page 10). These use cases should outline many of the common interactions that your users will have with your software. Simulating some of these use cases can be an excellent way to create highly representative benchmarks for your system.

Client-side benchmarks should be run in the target environment. If your marketing department tells you that your target platform is a 200MHz laptop with 48MB of RAM, you should have at least one of these machines for testing and benchmarking.

---

6. For more information about servlets and JavaServer Pages technology, see Larne Pekowsky, *JavaServer Pages.*™ Addison-Wesley, 2000.

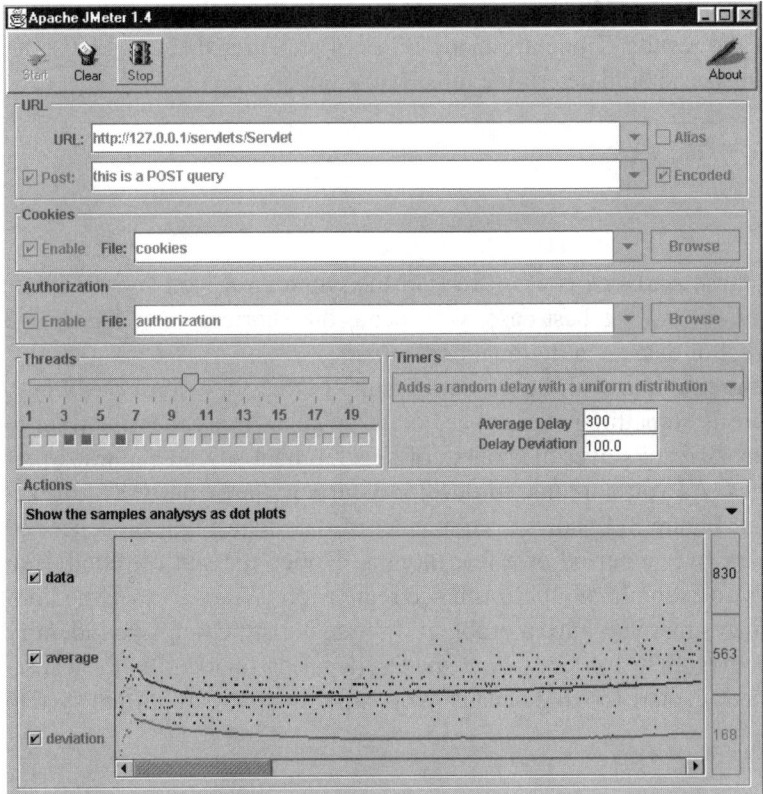

Figure 3-2   The `JMeter` testing application

3.1.4   Analyzing Benchmarks

Once you've created a set of benchmarks for your system, you need to be able to analyze and present the results. Keep in mind that benchmark results often vary from run to run. This happens for a number of reasons, such as background processing, network traffic, and general complexity. To help smooth the data and make it easier to analyze, it's often useful to run the benchmark several times.

You might want to run the benchmark inside the same VM invocation each time or kill the VM between each run. It depends on what you're measuring. If you're testing a task that happens only a few times while the program is running, it might make sense to run the benchmark in a separate VM each time. However, if you're testing a task that happens very often during the operation of the program, you should run the test in the same VM to allow for VM warm-up and to help identify global code interactions.

Once you have benchmark data for several runs, you'll need to perform statistical analysis of the results. There are many types of statistics that can be useful, but at a minimum you should determine three key numbers:

- Best case

- Worst case

- Average case

Computing these statistics is easy. To find the worst case, you simply locate the longest time. To find the best case, you locate the shortest time. Figure 3-3 shows a sample set of data for a fictional benchmark.

Of course, the problem with benchmark results is that they don't mean anything unless there is something to compare them against. You generally want to compare benchmark results over the course of development so you can track performance changes. As you continue to develop your software you want it to get faster, not slower. Figure 3-4 shows a sample set of data that might be generated by this benchmark over a period of a few months. Notice the spike around mid-February. This is an example of a performance regression. When you see the lines spike up, it indicates that you have a problem. Frequent testing helps you identify problems when they first appear, which makes it easier to identify the cause. You'll know where to start looking because you can tell what parts of the system have changed.

Run Number	Time
1	700 ms
2	720 ms
3	500 ms
4	400 ms
5	450 ms
Average	554 ms
Best	400 ms
Worst	720 ms

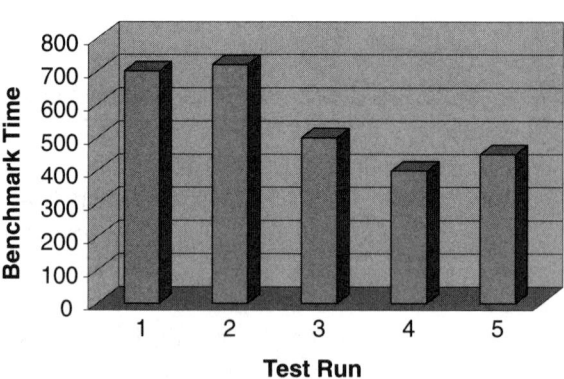

Figure 3-3   Benchmark results

Date	Best	Average	Worst
1/1	400 ms	554 ms	720 ms
1/8	405 ms	552 ms	725 ms
1/15	425 ms	555 ms	740 ms
1/22	380 ms	530 ms	700 ms
1/29	400 ms	532 ms	685 ms
2/5	380 ms	520 ms	700 ms
2/12	460 ms	580 ms	850 ms
2/19	375 ms	510 ms	700 ms
2/26	390 ms	515 ms	660 ms
3/5	360 ms	480 ms	650 ms
3/12	355 ms	480 ms	655 ms

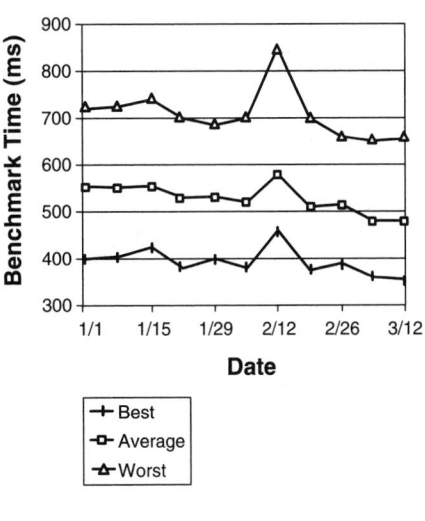

Figure 3-4   Tracking benchmark results

3.2   Profiling

Measuring method execution times by hand is fine when you suspect a particular method is slow. However, it is more difficult, and usually more important, to find the performance bottlenecks (also known as *hot spots*) in your program. This is where profiling tools come in. There are many profiling tools available—some are included with the Java 2 SDK, and others are stand-alone commercial products. (For more information about profiling tools, see *http://java.sun.com/docs/books/ performance.*)

A good profiling tool should be able to provide answers to the following questions:

- What methods are called most often?
- What methods are using the largest percentage of time?
- What methods are calling the most-used methods?
- What methods are allocating a lot of memory?

Commercial stand-alone profiling tools usually include sophisticated user interfaces that allow you to sort and slice your profile data in different ways.

HotSpot™ or hot spot?

The term *hot spot* is often used by programmers to describe a piece of code that takes up a large percentage of a program's total execution time. The Java HotSpot virtual machine is Sun Microsystems' advanced JVM implementation. The HotSpot VM provides a dynamic optimizing compiler that looks for hot spots in a program and automatically improves their performance as the program is running—this is where it gets its name. For more information about the HotSpot VM, see Appendix B.

Many SDKs also include basic profiling tools. For example, Sun's implementation of the Java 2 SDK version 1.2 includes an option called `hprof` that can be quite useful.

Warning: The profiling tools in the Java 2 SDK are `-X` options, which means the details of their use are subject to change.

3.2.1   Profiling Execution Times

Many programs spend the majority of their time executing just a few methods. A profiler can help you identify these hot spots so you can target your performance tuning efforts more effectively.

For example, you could use the Java 2 heap profiler, `hprof`, to find out where your program is spending its time. To profile a program with the Java 2 heap profiler, you invoke `hprof` and run the program from the command line:

```
java -Xhprof:cpu=y <MainClassName>
```

As the program runs, the profiler gathers data. When the program exits, it generates a large text file that contains the profile data. Figure 3-5 shows a snippet of the output generated by the profiler when typical user actions were simulated during the profiling session.

In the `hprof` output, the methods called by the program are ranked according to how much time was spent running the method. When you see data like this, you first need to look for patterns. For example, in Figure 3-5, there are multiple entries that include the word *font*. It seems a lot of time was spent manipulating fonts in this particular session.

```
CPU SAMPLES BEGIN (22043 samples) Tue April 18 20:50:57 2000
 rank   self  accum   trace method
   1    8.02%  8.02%  1212  sun/awt/font/NativeFontWrapper.getFontMetrics
   2    3.36% 11.38%   433  sun/awt/windows/WToolkit.eventLoop
   3    2.51% 13.90%  2065  sun/java2d/loops/ShortDiscreteRenderer.devSetRect
   4    1.99% 15.88%  1413  sun/awt/windows/WGraphics.W32LockViewResources
   5    1.89% 17.77%  1486  java/awt/GridBagLayout.preferredLayoutSize
   6    1.72% 19.49%  1216  sun/awt/font/NativeFontWrapper.getFontMetrics
   7    1.67% 21.16%  2386  sun/java2d/loops/DefaultComponent.ShortIsomorphicCopy
   8    1.33% 22.50%  1236  sun/awt/font/NativeFontWrapper.getAdvance
   9    1.29% 23.79%  2424  sun/awt/windows/WGraphics.W32UnLockViewResources
  10    1.14% 24.92%  2072  sun/java2d/loops/ShortDiscreteRenderer.devSetRect
```

Figure 3-5   Output from a profiler

Once you've figured out where the bottlenecks are, then you need to figure out what to do about them. In general, there are two approaches to optimization:

• Make often-used methods faster.
• Call slow methods less often.

These are both valid tactics, but programmers often fall into the trap of using only the first one. If you decide that you can make one of the methods in the list run faster, then by all means do that. However, you might be better off figuring out why that method is called so often, and reduce the number of times it is called.

Most profiling tools provide a way to backtrace from commonly called methods to determine which methods called them. Backtracing can lead to a better understanding of where the problems lie. For example, instead of spending days optimizing a certain calculation, you might gain more by caching the calculated value instead of recalculating it every time it's needed.

For example, consider the profile data in Figure 3-5. The method that was called most often is getFontMetrics. Who is calling it so often? Figure 3-6 shows a stack trace from the profiler that can help answer that question.

```
TRACE 1212:
 sun/awt/font/NativeFontWrapper.getFontMetrics(NativeFontWrapper.java:Native method)
 sun/awt/SunToolkit.getFontMetrics(SunToolkit.java:88)
 sun/awt/windows/WToolkit.getFontMetrics(WToolkit.java:338)
 com/meinc/java/framework/MyMenuItem.getPreferredMenuItemSize(MyMenuItem.java:245)
```

Figure 3-6   Profiler trace output

This is a backtrace from the biggest hot spot. It turns out that the FontMetrics are constantly being accessed in order to compute the preferred size of menu items! Now if you were the author of the MyMenuItem class, you could either (1) attempt to speed up the font metrics code, or (2) cache the preferred size of your menu item and only recalculate it when the font or menu item string changes. Option 2 is likely to yield better results.

3.2.2   Profiling Memory Usage

How your program handles memory usage is of critical importance to its overall performance. Traditionally, JVM implementations have made it quite expensive to allocate and reclaim memory. As a result, excessive memory allocation is often one of the first things that an experienced developer looks for when tuning a Java program. Removing unnecessary object allocations was one of the major tasks that the Swing team undertook in the process of developing the Swing 1.1 release. By using profiling tools to identify the places where large numbers of objects were being allocated, the team was able to speed up many commonly used operations by about 100 percent.

Newer runtimes, such as the HotSpot VM, have done a great deal to reduce the cost of allocating and collecting memory. However, there is still a cost associated with allocating an object. At a minimum, constructors for that object must be run and fields must be initialized—object allocation can never be free.

Because object creation can be expensive, many profiling tools provide data that can help track down areas where excessive memory allocation is taking place. Usually, profiling tools give you a way to find out what methods are allocating the most objects. There is often, but not always, a strong correlation between the methods that allocate large numbers of objects and the methods that are the hot spots in your program. It's often worth examining these methods to see if all of the allocations are necessary.

For example, you might find that you are allocating objects inside a loop when you actually only need one copy. Moving the allocation outside the loop will reduce memory consumption. In some cases, you might need only one instance of a particular object for your entire program. This is commonly referred to as the *Singleton pattern*[7] and is actually more common than it sounds.

---

7. For more information about the Singleton pattern, see Erich Gamma, et al., *Design Patterns: Elements of Reusable Object-Oriented Software*, pp. 127–134. Addison-Wesley, 1995.

3.2.3   Profiling to Locate Memory Leaks

Your software's RAM footprint can be of paramount importance to the overall performance and scalability of your system. One possible cause of large memory footprint problems is memory leaks. Although the virtual machine takes care of collecting unused objects, it is fairly simple to thwart the garbage collector through poor design or simple coding errors.

Broadly defined, a memory leak occurs anytime that memory is allocated, but not released when the programmer expects. In C++. the major cause of memory leaks is when objects are created with the keyword new, but are not freed with the delete keyword. If not explicitly freed, objects can continue to use heap space, even after all references to them in the program have been lost. These objects are called *dead bodies*, and they are a major problem in C++.

The Java programming language provides for automatic garbage collection (GC). This takes care of most of the common types of memory leaks encountered by C++ programs. You never have to explicitly free objects. Instead, when all references to an object are gone, the garbage collector removes the object for you. However, this doesn't mean that Java programs can't have memory leaks. Memory leaks occur when references to objects exist that the programmer has overlooked.

Isolating memory leaks can be a time-consuming, tedious, and difficult task. This is where profiling tools are helpful. Good profiling tools enable you to:

- Track the number of instances of all classes that exist at any given time.

- Isolate a particular object and view all of the references that point to it.

- Manually request garbage collection.

Different commercial tools implement these functions differently, but no matter what tool you use, the general process of debugging a memory leak is similar.

1. Determine that there is a leak.

2. Isolate objects that are leaking.

3. Trace references to leaking objects to determine what is holding them in memory.

Determining that there is a leak is generally fairly simple. The question to ask is: as your program executes, does it continue to use more and more memory? If your program's memory usage tends to increase, then drop back down to normal, it is behaving normally. (The GC mechanism is asynchronous.) However, if the program's memory usage continues to increase, then there's likely a memory leak. (See Chapter 5 for information about how to measure the amount of memory your program is using.)

Once you've determined that there's a leak, you need to isolate the leaking objects. To do this, you need a memory-profiling tool. Most commercial performance profiling tools also offer memory-profiling capabilities.

The first step in isolating the leak is to start the program and get it into a *warm state*. To do this, you need to perform several common operations to make sure that all of the one-time initialization costs are accounted for and all necessary classes are loaded. The next step is to get your program into a *known state* that you can return to later. For example, let's say you suspect you have a memory leak in your word processor. You could get it into a warm state by launching it, opening several documents, typing, copying, and pasting text. Then, to get it into a known state, you could close all of the open documents. The important thing is to be able to get the program into this exact same state later for comparison.

Once the program is in a warm, known state, you can use a profiling tool to determine the number of instances that exist of each class. To do this, manually request garbage collection and count the number of instances that remain. Most profiling tools have a button that requests the VM to process any available garbage and a Mark button that stores the number of instances of each class.

Now, exercise your program further and then return to your known state. For the word processor, this would mean opening more documents, typing, copying, and pasting, and then closing all of the open documents. Then return to the profiler, manually request garbage collection, and compare the number of instances that remain with the previous number. If the program doesn't have any memory leaks, the numbers should be the same. (In practice, there might be some small variances, such as small numbers of commonly copied objects such as rectangles or events.) If there's a leak, you'll likely see that there are more instances of several classes than there were the first time. For example, if the word processor has a leak, you might find that a number of `java.awt.Frame` or `javax.swing.JFrame` objects have accumulated in memory. Since you closed all of the documents to return the word processor to its known state, there shouldn't be any.

Once you've isolated an object that is leaking, select it and trace all of the references to it. You can then follow the reference chain back to the root cause of your memory leak. For more information about how to do this, refer to the documentation for your profiling tool. For more information about garbage collection, see Appendix A, The Truth About Garbage Collection.

3.3   Dealing with Flat Profiles

There is a relatively common hurdle to overcome when using a profiler: flat profiles. Generally, when you start tuning there are a few obvious hot spots that you can work on improving. However, eliminating the first few hot spots isn't always enough to make your program's performance meet your goals.

After the first pass at tuning, however, it often becomes harder to see patterns in the data—the profiles become flat, where no methods show up as easy-to-identify hot spots. For example, Table 3-2 shows some profiling data from a theoretical program. As you can see, there are no obvious hot spots in this program.

Looking at Table 3-2, you can see that `method3` and `method1` take more time than the other methods, but not significantly more. What you would like to see is a clearer indication of where you should spend your time tuning. Fortunately, most good profiling tools can provide additional data. The Time column in Table 3-2 shows the amount of time spent in each method. In addition to that, profilers often report a Cumulative Time value. This value indicates how much time was spent in that method, and any methods it calls. Table 3-3 shows the same data as Table 3-2, but adds a column for Cumulative Time.

What Table 3-3 shows is that although `method7` is only using a small fraction of the time itself, it is using a big block of time when you include the methods it calls. It can be hard to visualize exactly what this means from a table of data. Fortunately, many tools can provide a graphical view of this data. Figure 3-7 shows the same data as Table 3-3, represented as a *call tree*. The number in parentheses is the cumulative time spent in each method; this is the sum of the cumulative time spent in each method it calls. When the data is represented this way, it is easy to see that most of the work done by this program is triggered by calling `method7`.

Method Name	Time
method3	2
method1	2
main	1
method2	1
method5	1
method4	1
method8	1
method7	1
method6	1

Table 3-2   Flat Profile

Method Name	Cumulative Time	Time
main	11	1
method7	7	1
method3	2	2
method1	2	2
method2	2	1
method4	2	1
method6	2	1
method5	1	1
method8	1	1

Table 3-3   Profiling Cumulative Time

Profiling Execution Times on page 28 discussed an example involving menus and fonts and presented two basic strategies for tuning based on profiler data:

- Make often-used methods faster.
- Call slow methods less often.

These guidelines also apply when you're working with cumulative time data. In this example, you could either choose to reduce how often main calls method7, or speed up method7. Speeding up method7 would probably involve restructuring how it does its work. This might mean changing the algorithm or data structure used by method7, and the methods it calls. It also might require changes to your

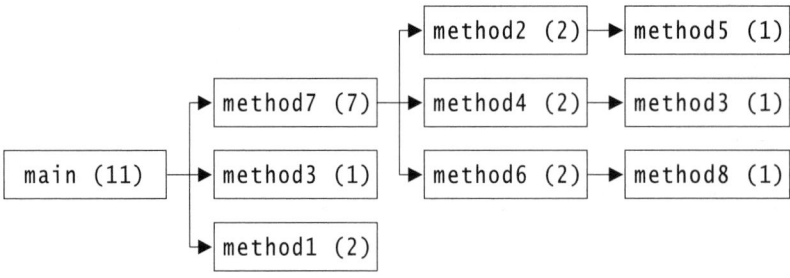

Figure 3-7   Graphical cumulative time view

object-oriented design. Remember that what you learn while profiling feeds back into your analysis and design, as well as your code.

3.3.1 A Flat Profile Example

A real-world example of this two-step tuning process was used for tuning Swing's JTable component. During the initial tuning, a lot of emphasis was placed on the obvious hot spots in the profile. These were mostly leaf nodes on the cumulative time tree. This led to some substantial speedups—around two times faster in many cases. This batch of tuning became part of the Swing 1.1 release and was a solid improvement, but it still wasn't fast enough for some users.

The problem that the Swing team faced was that there were no more glaring hot spots—or at least there were none that looked possible to fix given existing resource constraints and schedules. After spending considerable time struggling with this problem, it became apparent that when execution time was viewed on a cumulative basis there still were tunable hot spots.

For example, although the rendering speed of the JTable itself was vastly improved, the way that the JTable was updated during scrolling by the JViewport that contained it was a major bottleneck. Even though almost no time was spent in the code for JViewport, it was possible to substantially improve performance by redesigning the implementation of that class. In fact, after JViewport was redesigned to put fewer burdens on its contained components, scrolling speed improved by up to three times. This was one of the most popular performance enhancements in the J2SE 1.3 release.

Key Points

- Benchmarking is the science of quantitatively comparing two processes. Benchmarks are typically time-related, but can also measure quantities such as how much memory is used.

- You should create custom benchmarks to measure the performance of your own code.

- Benchmarks are good for comparing implementation choices, providing repeatable profiling cases, and tracking progress over time.

- Micro-benchmarks are useful, but don't always reflect real-world behavior.

- Macro-benchmarks help identify global interactions and usage patterns that affect performance.

- Profiling is the process of using a tool to better understand where your program is using the most resources.

- Profiling tools can give you data about CPU and RAM usage.

- Speeding up slow methods and calling slow methods less often are the two primary techniques for removing bottlenecks.

- Good profiling tools can help you find memory leaks.

- Viewing a profiler's timing data as cumulative time can help identify hot spots when profiles appear flat.

Part II: Tactics

tac•tic (tak´ tik), n. a method or maneuver to achieve a goal.

—Random House Webster's Dictionary

THIS part provides several tactics you can use to improve the performance of your software once you've figured out where the hot spots are.

The tactics described in this section are the result of empirical testing and the Java Software performance team's years of cumulative tuning experience. While they represent what we believe to be best programming practices, none of these tactics should be applied blindly. You should always measure your software's performance and analyze the results before and after performing any optimizations.

Most of the examples in this section include small benchmarks that illustrate the trade-offs associated with different solutions. Micro-benchmarks like these help you quickly evaluate the performance characteristics of a possible solution. Keep in mind, however, that micro-benchmarks won't reveal macro-level behaviors that might be equally important. You should create and run your own benchmarks to test the results of your optimizations.

Note: This section often cites benchmark results measured in milliseconds. These results are only representative of the configuration on which they were run. Factors such as the CPU, hard disk, operating system, and JVM can all impact performance—the same benchmarks run under different configurations might show substantially different results.

There are a nearly infinite number of optimizations that could be discussed in a performance book like this one. We've chosen to focus on tactics that we've seen used successfully in real-world projects. The tactics described here reflect lessons learned from tuning code in the libraries shipped with the JRE and from helping commercial software developers tune their applications. Our goal was to provide a field manual of battle-tested tactics, rather than an encyclopedic reference of possible techniques.

Clearly, many other useful techniques exist that are not covered here. Over time, we plan to make descriptions of additional tactics available online at *http://java.sun.com/docs/books/performance.*

Chapter 4, I/O Performance (page 41)
Programs of all types frequently need to input and output data, and I/O bottlenecks are a common performance issue. This chapter discusses how to take full advantage of the `java.io` package and avoid common coding errors that can lead to poor performance.

Chapter 5, RAM Footprint (page 53)
If it's too large, the amount of memory that a program uses can adversely affect performance. This chapter shows you how to measure the amount of memory a program uses and discusses the factors that affect memory consumption.

Chapter 6, Controlling Class Loading (page 67)
Loading a large number of classes can greatly increase a program's RAM footprint and slow its start-up time. This chapter presents three different techniques for reducing RAM footprint by reducing the number of classes that are loaded.

Chapter 7, Object Mutability: Strings and Other Things (page 85)
The choices you make when handling objects need to take into account their mutability—whether or not they can be changed. This chapter discusses different ways to avoid creating a large number of intermediate objects when using both mutable and immutable objects. Minimizing the number of intermediate objects can greatly improve a program's efficiency by eliminating the allocation, initialization, and collection of those objects.

Chapter 8, Algorithms and Data Structures (page 103)
Selecting the algorithm or data structure best-suited to a particular task is one of the keys to writing high-performance software. This chapter discusses how to select and evaluate algorithms and data structures for a particular task. It also addresses how some of the conventional wisdom about algorithms applies to the Java language and highlights some of the capabilities of the data structures and algorithms built into the Java 2 platform.

Chapter 9, Using Native Code (page 129)
Java developers have often resorted to native C code to try to achieve peak performance. This chapter discusses the actual performance costs and benefits associated with native code and when using native code is a reasonable option.

Chapter 10, Swing Models and Renderers (page 145)

To create highly interactive user interfaces for Java programs, you use the JFC Swing toolkit. This chapter looks at the Swing architecture and shows how you can get the best possible performance when using Swing's models and renderers.

Chapter 11, Writing Responsive User Interfaces with Swing (page 161)

Unresponsive user interfaces are among the most obvious types of performance problems. This chapter provides a set of guidelines and tactics for designing GUIs that provide fast, sensible responses to users' input.

Chapter 12, Deployment (page 183)

How you deploy your program generally has little or no effect on your code, but it can have a large impact on the user-perceived performance of your product. This chapter discusses different deployment strategies and presents several techniques for reducing the download time of network-based applications and applets.

CHAPTER 4

I/O Performance

BOTH client and server programs often use the java.io package. While this package is designed with ease of use in mind, developers new to the platform often make mistakes that can lead to poor I/O performance. Fortunately, a better understanding of this package can lead to major improvements in I/O performance.

Section 4.1 provides a brief overview of the java.io package, identifies the most common cause of poor I/O performance, and describes several different approaches to solving this problem. Section 4.2 focuses on object serialization, a key part of many of the newest features in the Java platform.

4.1   Basic I/O

Two abstract classes shape the architecture of the java.io package: InputStream and OutputStream. These interfaces define the key abstractions for I/O operations. Concrete implementations of InputStream and OutputStream provide access to different types of data sources such as disks and network connections.

The java.io package also provides several *filter* streams that don't point to a specific data source and are meant to be stacked on top of other streams. These filter streams are at the heart of the java.io architecture. From a performance perspective, the most interesting filter streams are buffered streams. Figure 4-1 shows a simplified class hierarchy that includes the buffered streams.

4.1.1   Buffered Streams

The leading cause of poor I/O performance is failing to buffer I/O operations. Hard disks are very good at reading and writing sizable chunks of data, but they are much less efficient when working with small blocks of data. To maximize I/O performance, you should batch read and write operations. This is exactly what buffered streams are designed for.

By default, most of the streams provided in the Java libraries write one byte of data at a time. Instead of putting buffering behavior into each individual stream

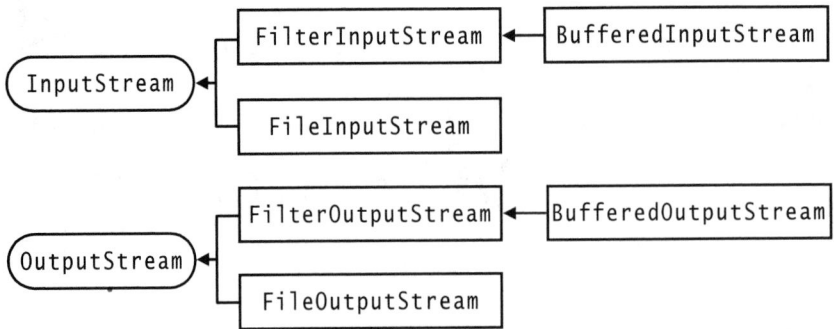

Figure 4-1   Simplified java.io class hierarchy

type, the buffering behavior is implemented in dedicated BufferedInputStream and BufferedOutputStream classes. This is very different from C, where the basic stdio operations are buffered by default. To better understand the effects of buffering streams, look at Listing 4-1. This example copies a file from one location to another.

```
public static void copy(String from, String to) throws IOException{
    InputStream in = null;
    OutputStream out = null;
    try {
        in = new FileInputStream(from);
        out = new FileOutputStream(to);
        while (true) {
            int data = in.read();
            if (data == -1) {
                break;
            }
            out.write(data);
        }
        in.close();
        out.close();
    } finally {
        if (in != null) {
            in.close();
        }
        if (out != null) {
            out.close();
        }
    }
}
```

Listing 4-1   Simple file copy

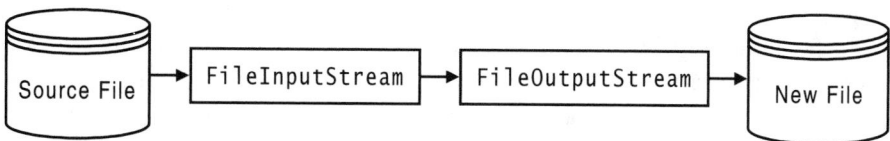

Figure 4-2 Copying with basic streams

The copy method opens a `FileInputStream` and a `FileOutputStream` and copies the contents of one directly into the other. Since the `read` and `write` methods work on individual bytes, this means an actual disk read and write occurs for each byte copied. Figure 4-2 illustrates how the data moves from one file to the other.

When the code in Listing 4-1 is run on our test configuration to copy a 370K JPEG test image, it takes almost 11 seconds to execute. Listing 4-2 shows a slightly modified version of the same code that uses buffered streams to improve performance. This code stacks buffered streams on top of the bare file streams. The buffered streams save up read and write requests and then execute them all at once—usually batching several thousand tiny requests into one larger request. When the code in Listing 4-2 is used to copy the same JPEG test file, it executes in a mere 130 milliseconds—almost 100 times faster!

```java
public static void copy(String from, String to) throws IOException{
    InputStream in = null;
    OutputStream out = null;
    try {
        InputStream inFile = new FileInputStream(from);
        in = new BufferedInputStream(inFile);
        OutputStream outFile = new FileOutputStream(to);
        out = new BufferedOutputStream(outFile);
        while (true) {
            int data = in.read();
            if (data == -1) {
                break;
            }
            out.write(data);
        }
    } finally {
        if (in != null) {
            in.close();
        }
        if (out != null) {
            out.close();
        }
    }
}
```

Listing 4-2 Faster file copy

Figure 4-3 shows how the data flows from one file to another when you're using buffers. Although using buffered streams is much faster than using bare file streams, you can see from Figure 4-3 that the buffers add a level of indirection. This does add some overhead and in some cases it's possible to improve performance by implementing a custom buffering scheme.

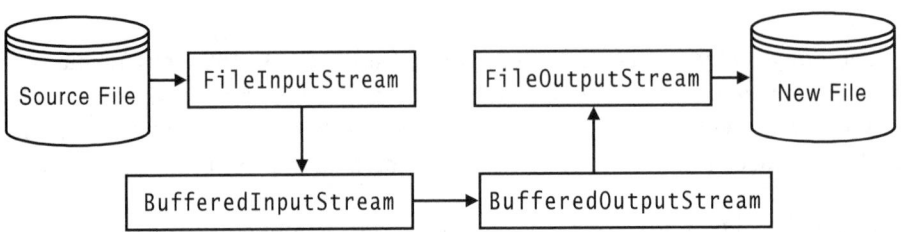

Figure 4-3   Copying with buffered streams

4.1.2   Custom Buffering

Copying data from one array to another using a `while` loop isn't as fast as you'd like it to be. Because the JVM enforces bounds checking, there is a good deal of overhead associated with such operations. When you're using buffered streams as shown in Listing 4-2, you essentially end up copying a lot of data from one array to another—several times, in fact. A large number of method calls are also made, many of them `synchronized`, with arguments that are passed and copied on the stack. Much of this overhead can be avoided, while still taking advantage of the fact that hard disks are good at reading and writing large chunks of data.

Listing 4-3 shows the `copy` method rewritten to use a custom buffering scheme. This block of code takes advantage of the fact that the `read` and `write` methods in `InputStream` and `OutputStream` are overloaded to work with `byte` arrays as well as individual bytes.

```
public int read();
public int read(byte[] bytes);

public void write();
public void write(byte[] bytes);
```

These methods allow you to work with large chunks of data, instead of just single bytes. In Listing 4-3 the code creates its own buffer, in the form of a `byte[]`, which it then uses to map the entire file into memory with a single `read` call. It then uses just one call to the `write` method to create the newly copied file.

```
public static void copy(String from, String to) throws IOException{
    InputStream in = null;
    OutputStream out = null;
    try {
        in = new FileInputStream(from);
        out = new FileOutputStream(to);
        int length = in.available(); // danger!
        byte[] bytes = new byte[length];
        in.read(bytes);
        out.write(bytes);
    } finally {
        if (in != null) {
            in.close();
        }
        if (out != null) {
            out.close();
        }
    }
}
```

Listing 4-3   Custom buffered copy

This code is very fast. Where the previous buffered stream version took about 130 milliseconds to copy the JPEG test file, using the single read and write operations reduces the time to about 33 milliseconds.

Note that there are two trade-offs to consider when using this strategy. First, this code creates a buffer the size of the original source file. If this code is used to copy large files, the buffer can get very large (perhaps larger than your available RAM). Second, this code creates a new buffer for each copy operation. If this code is used to copy a large number of files, the JVM has to allocate and collect many of these potentially large buffers. This is going to hurt performance.

It is possible to create a version of the custom buffered copy that avoids these two pitfalls and is even faster. To do this, you create a single, static buffer and then read or write blocks the size of that buffer. This results in more than one read or write operation for files larger than the buffer, but the cost is offset by the fact that a fresh buffer doesn't have to be allocated for each file that is copied. (The costs of such allocations are discussed further in Chapter 7, Object Mutability: Strings and Other Things.) The size of the buffer is known and can be optimized to achieve the best trade-off between speed and memory-use for each particular situation.

Listing 4-4 shows the code for the improved custom buffered copy function. In this version, a static 100K buffer is used for the copy operation. For copying the same JPEG test file, this implementation is even faster than the one in Listing 4-3. This is because a new buffer doesn't have to be allocated for every copy.

```
static final int BUFF_SIZE = 100000;
static final byte[] buffer = new byte[BUFF_SIZE];

public static void copy(String from, String to) throws IOException{
    InputStream in = null;
    OutputStream out = null;
    try {
        in = new FileInputStream(from);
        out = new FileOutputStream(to);
        while (true) {
            synchronized (buffer) {
                int amountRead = in.read(buffer);
                if (amountRead == -1) {
                    break;
                }
                out.write(buffer, 0, amountRead);
            }
        }
    } finally {
        if (in != null) {
            in.close();
        }
        if (out != null) {
            out.close();
        }
    }
}
```

Listing 4-4   Improved custom buffered copy

One key item to note in Listing 4-4 is the synchronized block. In a single threaded environment, this code will work fine without the synchronized block. However, if you want to use this code in a multithreaded environment, you need to synchronize the buffer to prevent multiple threads from trying to write to it simultaneously. Although there are costs associated with synchronization, there is almost no performance impact because the number of iterations through the while loop is small. In our tests, both synchronized and unsynchronized versions of this code took the same amount of time to copy the test file.

Table 4-1 shows the approximate copy times for the different copy tactics. While the results from such micro-benchmarks don't show the whole performance picture, they provide a rough idea of how the different options compare.

Strategy	Time
Raw File Streams	10800 ms
Buffered Streams	130 ms
Custom Buffer	33 ms
Custom Buffer 2	22 ms

Table 4-1 Copy Times

4.1.3   Further Improvements

Typically, there are application-specific ways to further improve I/O performance. By examining an application's purpose and operation, you can often find opportunities for big performance improvements.

For example, consider an FTP or HTTP server. The primary job of such a server is to copy files from a disk to a network socket. Although a server might have access to thousands of files, a small fraction of these files typically represent the majority of the files served. A web site's main homepage is probably served much more often than other pages in the site. To improve performance, you could implement your server so that the most commonly accessed files are mapped into cached byte[] structures. That way, those files don't need to be read from disk each time; they can be copied directly from memory to the network socket.

4.2   Serialization

Object serialization is the process through which live objects are flattened into a form that can be written to and read from a stream. These flattened objects can be piped into files or even sent across a network. Together, object serialization and the Java platform's hardware-independent byte-codes enable revolutionary software solutions, such as advanced distributed system software and mobile agent software. Technologies such as Remote Method Invocation (RMI), and in turn Jini™ technology, rely on serialization. The java.io package provides classes that support object serialization.

One of the best features of serialization is that it is almost completely automatic. It takes very little work to use serialization to make your objects persistent—in general, all you need to do is implement the Serializable interface.

The outward simplicity of the serialization API hides its internal complexity. The internal machinery that enables transparent object serialization is very complex and can be quite costly at runtime. Fortunately, there are tactics you can use to mitigate these costs.

4.2.1   Serialization Example

The `Serializable` interface is actually purely a tagging interface—it doesn't define any methods. `Serializable` is simply used to indicate that the class is designed to be serialized. Listing 4-5 shows a simple class that implements the `Serializable` interface.

```
public class TestObject implements Serializable {

    private int value;
    private String name;
    private Date timeStamp;
    private JPanel panel;

    public TestObject(int value) {
        this.value = value;
        name = new String("Object:" + value);
        timeStamp = new Date();
        panel = new JPanel();
        panel.add(new JTextField());
        panel.add(new JButton("Help"));
        panel.add(new JLabel("This is a text label"));
    }
}
```

Listing 4-5   Simple serializable class

Because this class implements the `Serializable` interface and the instance variables are serializable, any instance of this class can be written to an `ObjectOutputStream`. Listing 4-6 shows a code fragment that creates 50 instances of the `TestObject` class and writes them to an `ObjectOutputStream`.

```
for (int i =0;i <50; i++) {
    vector.addElement(new TestObject(i));
}
Stopwatch timer = new Stopwatch().start();
try {
    OutputStream file = new FileOutputStream("Out.test");
    OutputStream buffer = new BufferedOutputStream(file);
    ObjectOutputStream out = new ObjectOutputStream(buffer);
    out.writeObject(vector);
    out.close();
} catch (Exception e) {
    e.printStackTrace();
```

```
}
timer.stop();
System.out.println("elapsed = " + timer.getElapsedTime());
```

Listing 4-6   Writing objects to a stream

Once you've streamed these objects to disk, you can re-create them using an
`ObjectInputStream`. Listing 4-7 shows a code fragment that loads objects from a
file.

```
Stopwatch timer = new Stopwatch().start();
try {
   InputStream file = new FileInputStream("Out.test");
   InputStream buffer = new BufferedInputStream(file);
   ObjectInputStream in = new ObjectInputStream(buffer);
   vector = (Vector)in.readObject();
   in.close();
} catch (Exception e) {
   e.printStackTrace();
}
timer.stop();
System.out.println("elapsed = " + timer.getElapsedTime());
```

Listing 4-7   Reading objects from a stream

When the file created by writing a `Vector` that contains 50 of these test objects is written to disk, the resulting file occupies about 91K. That's almost 2K per
instance of the class. That seems like a lot, considering the entire source file that
defines the class takes up only about 500 bytes. Clearly, there is a lot of stuff being
written into these files. This stems from the fact that serialization is a recursive
process. When a single object is serialized, the `ObjectOutputStream` examines all
the object's fields (even the private ones) and writes them out. If the fields contain
other objects, those are also written out, and so on.

In the `TestObject` example, all of the Swing UI widgets and any objects they
reference are written out along with the `TestObject`. Even fields set to the same
value that is set by the class's default constructor are written out, because serialization has no knowledge of the default values for fields.

4.2.2   Improved Serialization Example

The good news is that the serialization mechanism provides tools that give you
better control over what's written out. The primary tool for this is the `transient`
keyword. This keyword allows you to specify values that are noncritical, or that
can be reconstructed manually after the object is read into memory.

Listing 4-8 shows a new version of the TestObject class that uses the transient keyword to specify that two of the four fields defined by the class should not to be written out by the ObjectOutputStream. It also defines a private method called readObject. The ObjectInputStream class looks for a method with this signature (using machinery from within the JVM) and automatically calls this method while reading the object in, even though it is private. This hook can be used to reinitialize transient state in your object after it has been reconstructed from a stream. In this example, the user interface panel and the name are reinitialized after the class is read in. This dramatically improves performance for both reading and writing.

```
public class TestObjectTrans implements Serializable {

    private int value;
    private transient String name;
    private DatetimeStamp;
    private transient JPanel panel;

    public TestObjectTrans(int value) {
        this.value = value;
        timeStamp = new Date();
        initTransients();
    }

    public void initTransients() {
        name = new String("Object:" + value);
        panel = new JPanel();
        panel.add(new JTextField());
        panel.add(new JButton("Help"));
        panel.add(new JLabel("This is a text label"));
    }

    private void readObject(ObjectInputStream in)
                throws IOException, ClassNotFoundException {
        in.defaultReadObject();
        initTransients();
    }
}
```

Listing 4-8   Improved serializable object

Table 4-2 shows a comparison between the TestObject implementation and the modified version that uses the transient keyword to prevent selected fields from being written out.

	TestObject	**TestObjectTrans**
Save Time	990 ms	110 ms
Load Time	3,680 ms	1,040 ms
File Size	91.7K	1.6K

Table 4-2   Serialization Comparison

As you can see, using the `transient` keyword drastically improves the performance of serializing these objects:

- The time to flatten and save 50 of these objects was reduced by nine times.

- The time to load and reconstruct the objects was reduced by four times.

- The size of the resulting file was reduced by more than 50 times.

Note that this last figure is especially crucial if you are piping these objects over a
network instead of just to a local file. Making a change like this in an application
that uses RMI to move objects could result in a significant reduction in network
traffic.

4.2.3   Analyzing Persistent State

If your software depends on the serialization mechanism, then you need to perform some analysis to determine what object state information needs to be persistent and what can be recalculated after an object has been reconstituted.

In the example in Listing 4-8, streaming out a simple object causes several
Swing user interface components to be streamed out as well. While this example
might seem artificial, it's actually a simplified version of a problem encountered
by a group of developers who were working on a server program.

When the server process needed to be terminated, the program serialized a set
of important objects and streamed them to a file. When the server was restarted,
this enabled it to re-create these objects and begin running in the same state where
it left off. The problem was that it took more than 30 minutes to stream these
objects to disk, which was clearly unacceptable. When the developers analyzed
the required persistent state of their objects, they found many things were being
streamed that didn't need to be. In fact, because of the recursive nature of serialization, almost the entire object heap was being streamed to disk. Careful use of
the `transient` keyword drastically reduced the time it took to write out their data.

Key Points

- Reading and writing data in small chunks can be very slow.
- Using `BufferedInputStream` and `BufferedOutputStream` to batch requests improves performance.
- In some situations, you can use custom buffering techniques to maximize performance.
- Serialization can be very costly.
- Using the `transient` keyword reduces the amount of data serialized.

CHAPTER 5

RAM Footprint

A PROGRAM'S RAM footprint can be critical to its success. A program that uses too much memory can force the operating system to rely on virtual memory. Because virtual memory is many times slower than physical RAM, relying on virtual memory can result in slow performance and a poor user experience. While developing your system, be aware of your target deployment environment and consider how much RAM will be available on machines running your software.

Before you can optimize your program's footprint, it's important to understand how memory is used. There are many common misconceptions about how memory is consumed by Java programs, and it is easy to put a lot of effort into footprint control for relatively small gains. By understanding the factors that contribute to footprint, you can make informed decisions when coding.

This chapter shows you how to accurately measure the amount of memory used by your application and describes the factors that contribute to an application's RAM footprint. For tactics you can use to control some of these common problems, see Chapter 6, Controlling Class Loading.

5.1 Computing RAM Footprint

Figuring out how much RAM your program is consuming can be tricky. While the Java platform provides some facilities that help, they're not as useful as they first appear. To fully evaluate your program's footprint, you need to use platform-specific mechanisms. This section discusses the APIs that relate to memory usage and a few of the platform-specific utilities that you can use to measure footprint.

5.1.1 Assessing Memory Usage

Two methods in the `java.lang.Runtime` class can give you a general idea of how much memory is being consumed by your program. These methods look at the size of the virtual machine's object heap.

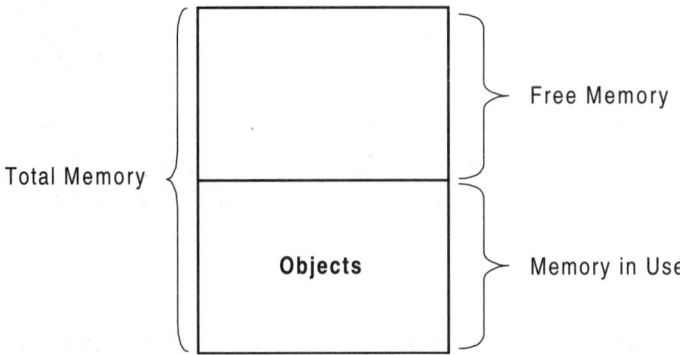

Figure 5-1   The object heap

- `Runtime.totalMemory`—returns the size (in bytes) of the heap used to allocate objects
- `Runtime.freeMemory`—returns the amount of memory not being used in the object heap

You can figure out approximately how much space objects are consuming by subtracting the `freeMemory` from the `totalMemory`. Figure 5-1 shows a simplified representation of the object heap. Note that the physical layout of the heap is totally implementation-dependent and can vary widely.

These memory inspection methods are useful in a number of situations. For example, you can use them to display your program's heap usage at regular intervals. If the heap usage continues to increase over time, you might have a memory leak.

Although these memory inspection methods are useful, they only measure the object heap. Objects are not the only things that contribute to a program's RAM footprint. The only thing you can say for sure about the relationship between the memory usage calculated with the `Runtime` methods and the actual amount of memory your program requires is that the actual requirements are much larger.

5.1.2   Measuring a Program's True Footprint

There are no methods in the standard API to help you assess the true footprint of your program. To accurately measure your program's total footprint, you need to use platform-specific utilities.

Microsoft Windows NT 4.0 provides a tool called the Task Manager that displays memory usage information for the processes that are currently running. This information provides a more complete picture of your program's total RAM footprint.

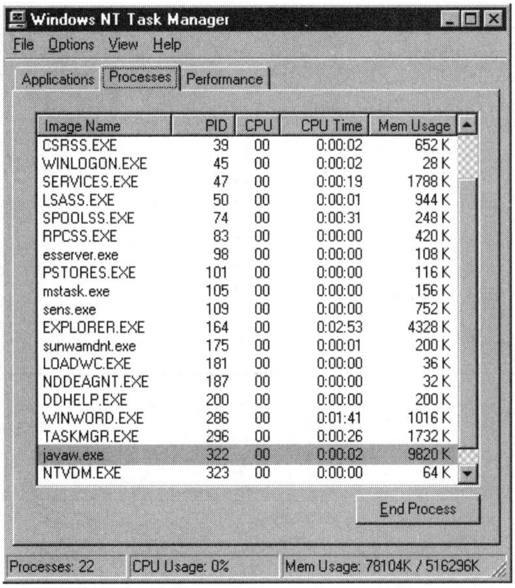

Figure 5-2   The Windows NT Task Manager

To access the Task Manager on Windows NT, type `ctrl-alt-del` and click the Task Manager button in the dialog that's displayed. In the Task Manager window, look for a process called something like `java.exe` or `javaw.exe`. The program shown in Figure 5-2 is consuming about 9.8MB of RAM.

On Solaris, you can use the command line driven `pmap` utility to view your program's memory usage. This utility prints a map of the process's address space. You have to pass `pmap` a process ID with the `-x` option. To find the process ID for your JVM, use the `ps` command. Figure 5-3 shows how to find a running virtual machine and measure its memory usage. The key information reported by `pmap` is the `total Kb` entry in the `Private` column. The program shown in Figure 5-3 is using approximately 22MB of RAM.

5.2   What Contributes to Footprint?

Given that the object heap is much smaller than the total memory consumed by most programs, where is the memory being used? Several factors contribute to the overall footprint of a program:

- Objects
- Classes

```
steve>ps -e | grep java
   4874 pts/12   0:18 java
steve>/usr/proc/bin/pmap -x 4874
4874:    /usr/local/java/jdk1.3/solaris/bin/../bin/sparc/native_threads/java HT
Address    Kbytes Resident Shared Private Permissions        Mapped File
00010000      24      24       8      16 read/exec           java
00024000       8       8       -       8 read/write/exec     java
  .
  .
  .
FF9F0000      24      24       -      24 -                    [ stack ]
FF9F6000    2024    2024       -    2024 read/write/exec      [ stack ]
--------  ------  ------  ------  ------
total Kb  158128   25296    3216   22080
```

Figure 5-3   Measuring footprint on Solaris

- Threads
- Native data structures
- Native code

The relative memory consumption associated with each item varies across applications, runtime environments, and platforms. For a particular program, any one of these items might be the number one memory consumer.

Objects and classes typically make up the bulk of a program's RAM footprint. The ratio between the two, however, is application-specific. Figure 5-4 shows the breakdown for two theoretical applications.

In small to mid-sized client-programs, objects don't usually use the bulk of the memory consumed; the memory is used by classes. It takes several hundred classes to start a small GUI program, even one that creates only a few buttons and text fields. This is important when you evaluate how to optimize the RAM footprint of your program. Reducing the number of classes loaded is often more

Small GUI Application

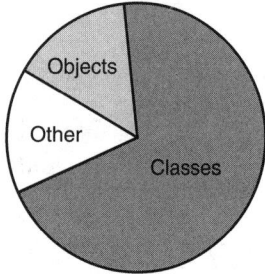

Large Server Application

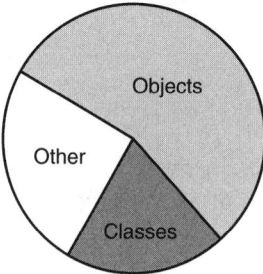

Figure 5-4   RAM consumption for two applications

important than reducing the number of objects. (See Chapter 6, Controlling Class Loading, for more information.)

5.2.1   Objects

In many ways, the number of objects used is the part of your program's footprint over which you have the most control. Often, however, the number of objects used isn't the biggest contributing factor to your program's footprint. You need to be able to estimate the size of an object and understand the impact it has on your overall footprint before you start trying to optimize.

The following section, Estimating the Size of an Object, provides a basic heuristic for quickly approximating the size of an object. The Measuring Object Size section shows a simple tool you can use to measure object size. Tactics for optimizing object size are described in the Optimizing Object Size section on page 61.

Estimating the Size of an Object
The exact size of any particular object isn't specifically defined in any of the Java platform specifications. However, it's fairly easy to roughly approximate the size of an object based on information such as the sizes of primitives in the Java programming language, which are shown in Table 5-1. With the exception of `reference`, primitive sizes are defined by the language specification and do not change.[1] The size of a `reference` isn't well defined, but it is typically 4 bytes on a 32-bit system and 8 bytes on a 64-bit system.

The heuristic for computing the approximate size of an object is

```
The sum of all fields + per object overhead
```

The amount of overhead associated with an object isn't defined, but 8 bytes is typical.

Data Type	Size
byte	1 byte
char	2 bytes
short	2 bytes

Table 5-1   Primitive Sizes

---

1. Technically, the sizes aren't specified. The size of these structures is implied by the number of bits required to represent the required range, but a runtime could use more memory if it chose.

Data Type	Size
`int`	4 bytes
`float`	4 bytes
`long`	8 bytes
`double`	8 bytes
"reference"	4 bytes (typically)

Table 5-1   Primitive Sizes

With this formula and the information in Table 5-1, it is possible to estimate an object's size. The exact amount of space used by the object depends on the virtual machine implementation, but this formula gives you something to work from. For example, the size of the object defined in Listing 5-1 can be estimated using the preceding formula.

```
class Cat {
    short lives = 9;
    double chanceToLandOnFeet = .998;
    Tail tail = null;
}
```

Listing 5-1   A simple class

The approximate size of a single instance of this class is

```
2 (short) + 8 (double) + 4 (reference) + 8 (overhead) = 22 bytes
```

Keep in mind that this is just an approximation of the object size—JVM implementations are free to structure their objects very differently. For example, a common optimization is to align all the fields on word boundaries (even if the field only requires a single byte of storage). This increases the size of many types of objects running on the JVM. The next section discusses a technique for measuring object size that makes some of these differences more apparent.

Measuring Object Size

While the Java platform doesn't provide a way to measure the size of an object, it is possible to measure the approximate size indirectly. Section 5.1.1 discusses the `Runtime` methods that provide information about the size of the JVM's object heap.

You can also use these methods to determine the approximate size of an object by:

1. Requesting garbage collection to get the heap into a known state.

2. Measuring the free heap space.

3. Creating an instance of the class you want to measure and keeping a reference to it.

4. Requesting garbage collection again.

5. Measuring the free heap space.

6. Subtracting the second measurement from the first.

Although this general approach works, it has some flaws:

- Garbage collection can be unpredictable.

- Caching performed by the class when the first instance is created can skew the results.

- The `Runtime.freeSpace` method might not be accurate down to the byte level.

Fortunately, you can get around most of these by:

- Creating a primer instance of the class before your measure the heap the first time. This eliminates the impact of one-time cache costs.

- Measuring several instances of the object and calculating the average. This helps offset the unpredictability inherent in the GC behavior and the heap space measurement methods.

Listing 5-2 contains the source code for a utility that implements these techniques. To use the utility, you pass the name of the class you want to measure to the `sizeOf` method. Instances of the specified class are created using reflection and measured.

```
public class ObjectScale {
    public static long sizeOf(Class clazz) {
        long size= 0;
        Object[] objects = new Object[100];
        try {
            Object primer = clazz.newInstance();
            long startingMemoryUse = getUsedMemory();
            for (int i = 0; i < objects.length; i++) {
                objects[i] = clazz.newInstance();
            }
            long endingMemoryUse = getUsedMemory();
```

```
            float approxSize = (endingMemoryUse -
                               startingMemory-Use) / 100f;
            size = Math.round(approxSize);
        } catch (Exception e) {
            System.out.println("WARNING:couldn't instantiate"
                               +clazz);
            e.printStackTrace();
        }
        return size;
    }
    private static long getUsedMemory() {
        gc();
        long totalMemory = Runtime.getRuntime().totalMemory();
        gc();
        long freeMemory = Runtime.getRuntime().freeMemory();
        long usedMemory = totalMemory - freeMemory;
        return usedMemory;
    }
    private static void gc() {
        try {
            System.gc();
            Thread.currentThread().sleep(100);
            System.runFinalization();
            Thread.currentThread().sleep(100);
            System.gc();
            Thread.currentThread().sleep(100);
            System.runFinalization();
            Thread.currentThread().sleep(100);
        } catch (Exception e) {
            e.printStackTrace();
        }
    }
    public static void main(String[] args) {
        try {
            Class clazz = Class.forName(args[0]);
            System.out.println(sizeOf(clazz));
        } catch (Exception e) {
            e.printStackTrace();
        }
        System.exit(0);
    }
}
```

Listing 5-2   Utility for measuring object size

Although this utility provides a reasonable estimate, it isn't 100 percent accurate. The size of a particular object can vary substantially under different JVM implementations.

Table 5-2 shows the sizes of several types of objects measured using the ObjectScale utility—note how the sizes vary across different versions of the

Class	Java 2 SDK 1.2.2	Java 2 SDK 1.3
`java.lang.Object`	16 bytes	8 bytes
`java.util.Hashtable`	472 bytes	96 bytes
`java.awt.Point`	24 bytes	16 bytes
`javax.swing.JTextField`	3,082 bytes	3,109 bytes
`javax.swing.JTable`	26,836 bytes	4,086 bytes

Table 5-2   Common Object Sizes

Java 2 SDK. In this case, these differences are due to performance tuning in 1.3, but object sizes can vary from release to release for a number of reasons.

The change in sizes from one release to the next is caused by a number of things. For example, the change in `Object` is due to decreased overhead in the virtual machine. The decrease in the size of `Hashtable` is due to a reduction in the default capacity of the internal data structure. The reduction in size of an instance of `JTable` is a combination of several factors, including the delayed initialization of some large structures only used by a small percentage of applications.

Optimizing Object Size

Developers sometimes try to reduce a program's RAM footprint by reducing the size of the objects that are instantiated. This can help, but it might not result in the savings you expect. For example, consider the class in Listing 5-3, a high-precision point class that might be used in a 3D modeling program to represent an exact location in space.

```
class FinePoint {
    double x;
    double y;
    double z;
}
```

Listing 5-3   High-precision point class

According to the heuristic described in the Estimating the Size of an Object section, an instance of this class consumes approximately 28 bytes. Since a 3D modeling program is likely to create a large number of these point objects, it might be tempting to sacrifice precision and switch from `double` to `float`. This would reduce the size of the object to about 16 bytes, a savings of 12 bytes per point. If a typical 3D model contains 5,000 points, you could save 60K with this optimization.

While this might seem like a pretty good improvement, 60K probably represents a very small percentage of the program's total footprint. If the program has a total RAM footprint of 12MB, the savings is only 0.5 percent of the total footprint. In this case, the loss in precision probably isn't worth the minor reduction in footprint—it would make more sense to look for more beneficial optimizations.

You should always do this type of calculation before you start trying to optimize the size of a particular object. Profiling tools can help you determine how many instances of a given class are in memory. By assessing the impact of the size of those objects on the overall footprint, you can make informed decisions about what to optimize.

5.2.2   Classes

Several entities associated with loaded classes contribute to RAM footprint:

- Bytecodes
- Reflective data structures
- Constant pool entries
- JIT compiled code

Bytecodes
When a source file is compiled with `javac` it produces a class file. Each method in the class is described by a set of bytecodes. This set of bytecodes is a processor neutral version of the machine code that executes on your computer's processor. When a class is loaded, the bytecodes for that class's methods must also be loaded so that when a method is executed the instructions are available to the virtual machine. These loaded bytecodes occupy space in RAM.

Reflective Data Structures
When a class is loaded by a virtual machine, two things happen:

1. The class file is loaded into RAM.
2. The contents of the file are parsed and reflective data structures are created inside the virtual machine to represent the class's methods and fields.

Typically, the JVM creates structures to represent each method and field within the class. The size of these structures is totally dependent on the JVM implementation. However, inspection of a variety of JVM implementations shows that the size of the reflective structures can be substantial.

Constant Pool Entries

The constants defined by a class also contribute to the program's footprint. For example, any string literal that appears in your code is stored in a special table. The names of all the classes, methods, and fields are also stored.

JIT Compiled Code

If the JIT stores compiled code for a large number of methods, it can lead to a major increase in footprint. Early JIT code generators converted each method into native code the first time it was called. While this drastically improved performance in some situations, it led to major problems in others. In particular, this approach leads to a major increase in footprint. It turns out that many program methods are executed very few times, while others are executed thousands of times. Converting all of the bytecodes resulted in native code being stored for a large number of methods that were never executed again. Newer JIT compilers use better rules to determine when to compile methods. Seldom-used methods are never compiled, which helps reduce the impact to the program's footprint.

5.2.3   Threads

The impact that threads have on RAM footprint isn't a problem for most programs, but running threads do need space to store their stack state, and the system-specific data structures do consume memory.

Because runtime implementations vary widely in how threads are handled, you might encounter situations where the impact threads have on footprint is significant. For example, some ports of the JRE create a heavyweight OS process for each running thread. In an application that uses many threads, this means that thread costs, rather than class or object costs, can become the dominant factor in the program's memory consumption.

You shouldn't avoid using threads—they're necessary in many cases, and generally don't have a large impact on footprint. However, you should be aware that the impact can be very different across runtimes. This is one of the reasons it's a good idea to measure performance characteristics under your program's different target environments.

5.2.4   Native Data Structures

Some classes in the Java libraries create native, OS-specific resources. In particular, AWT uses large numbers of native data structures. For example, most AWT components, such as `java.awt.Button`, require native peers. You should think about whether the classes you use are likely to require large native structures and consider the impact they could have on footprint.

It isn't always possible to tell that a class uses native structures just by looking at it, but one good indication is the presence of a `finalizer` method. If the class provides (or inherits) a `finalize` method, it is probably because the object needs to free native data structures before it is garbage collected. Finalizer methods also present other issues. See Appendix A, The Truth About Garbage Collection, for more information.

5.2.5   Native Libraries

Runtimes always depend on some native code, which often resides in shared libraries. For example, a particular runtime implementation might have shared libraries for the virtual machine, AWT, and networking. These libraries often have dependencies on standard libraries such as the C runtime library. Although these costs typically are out of your control, you should be aware that they exist so you have a complete picture of what's going on.

5.3   Class Loading

The key problem with classes, from a footprint perspective, is that you often load more than you need. Class loading is like a web—loading a single class often causes several others to be loaded, which in turn load more classes, and so on. The key is to try to load only what you use, and defer loading rarely-used features until they are needed. For more information about how to do this, see Chapter 6, Controlling Class Loading.

Before you start worrying about how to reduce the number of classes you load, though, you need to be able to measure what is being loaded.

5.3.1   Measuring Class Loads

To list each class as it's loaded, you can use the -verbose flag when you launch your program. For example:

```
java -verbose <MyMainClass>
```

A line is output to the console for each class that's loaded. Figure 5-5 shows a partial list of the classes loaded to run a simple spreadsheet application. One key piece of information this gives you is the number of classes required to start your

```
C:\spreadsheet>java -verbose Spreadsheet
 [Loaded java/lang/Thread.class from c:\jdk1.1.7a\lib\classes.zip]
 [Loaded java/lang/Object.class from c:\jdk1.1.7a\lib\classes.zip]
 [Loaded java/lang/Class.class from c:\jdk1.1.7a\lib\classes.zip]
 [Loaded java/lang/String.class from c:\jdk1.1.7a\lib\classes.zip]
 [Loaded java/io/Serializable.class from c:\jdk1.1.7a\lib\classes.zip]
 [Loaded java/lang/ThreadDeath.class from c:\jdk1.1.7a\lib\classes.zip]
 [Loaded java/lang/Error.class from c:\jdk1.1.7a\lib\classes.zip]
 [Loaded java/lang/Throwable.class from c:\jdk1.1.7a\lib\classes.zip]
 [Loaded java/lang/Exception.class from c:\jdk1.1.7a\lib\classes.zip]
 [Loaded java/lang/RuntimeException.class from c:\jdk1.1.7a\lib\classes.zip]
 [Loaded java/lang/Cloneable.class from c:\jdk1.1.7a\lib\classes.zip]
 [Loaded java/lang/Runnable.class from c:\jdk1.1.7a\lib\classes.zip]
 [Loaded java/lang/ThreadGroup.class from c:\jdk1.1.7a\lib\classes.zip]
 [Loaded java/lang/StringBuffer.class from c:\jdk1.1.7a\lib\classes.zip]
 [Loaded java/lang/System.class from c:\jdk1.1.7a\lib\classes.zip]
 [Loaded java/lang/Integer.class from c:\jdk1.1.7a\lib\classes.zip]
 [Loaded java/lang/Number.class from c:\jdk1.1.7a\lib\classes.zip]
 [Loaded java/lang/NoClassDefFoundError.class from c:\jdk1.1.7a\lib\classes.zip]
 [Loaded java/lang/LinkageError.class from c:\jdk1.1.7a\lib\classes.zip]
 [Loaded java/lang/OutOfMemoryError.class from c:\jdk1.1.7a\lib\classes.zip]
 [Loaded java/lang/VirtualMachineError.class from c:\jdk1.1.7a\lib\classes.zip]
 [Loaded java/util/Properties.class from c:\jdk1.1.7a\lib\classes.zip]
 [Loaded java/util/Hashtable.class from c:\jdk1.1.7a\lib\classes.zip]
 [Loaded java/util/Dictionary.class from c:\jdk1.1.7a\lib\classes.zip]
```

Figure 5-5 Partial class loads for a sample program

program. By simply counting the number of lines produced by the verbose output, you can see precisely how many classes are loaded.

By tracking the number of classes loaded as development progresses, you can catch potential problems early. For example, you might find that a particular change causes the number of classes loaded to increase sharply. It's much easier to track down the cause if you catch the increase when the change is introduced instead of trying to address class loading issues at the end of the development cycle.

Key Points

- RAM footprint can be the key, limiting factor on performance, especially in environments with limited memory.

- You need to understand where memory is being consumed before you can optimize effectively.

- You can use the `Runtime` methods to measure object heap, but platform-specific tools are needed to measure true footprint.

- Objects, loaded classes, threads, and native data structures can all contribute to RAM footprint.

CHAPTER **6**

Controlling Class Loading

LOADING too many classes can have a significant impact on the RAM footprint of your program. Fortunately, there are a number of techniques you can use to reduce the number of classes that are loaded.

This chapter discusses three tactics for controlling class loading. Interestingly, all three tactics rely on the Java language's dynamic reflection features. While reflection isn't as fast as normal method dispatch, in many cases the benefits of using reflection outweigh the slight reduction in speed.

These reflection-based techniques aren't general-purpose solutions—they're designed to solve specific problems relating to class loading and footprint. As with most of the tactics presented in this book, you should carefully evaluate whether or not they are relevant to your application and measure the effects of your changes. In some cases, you might need to balance the requirements that your program should be robust and maintainable against small performance gains.

The three techniques discussed here offer varying degrees of improvement in the amount of RAM classes consume in your program. These techniques can help with the following problems:

- Eager class loading
- The creation of too many small classes
- The lack of sharing between virtual machine instances

6.1   Eager Class Loading

Obviously, a class needs to be loaded before an instance of that class can be created. However, many factors can cause a class to be loaded before you think it should be. For example, some JIT compilers cause all classes referenced by a method to be loaded before that method can be compiled. Security measures such as the verifier can also eagerly load classes.

To better understand this problem, consider a simple word processing program. A major feature of such a program is the ability to open and display a wide range of document types. The program could be designed with an elegant

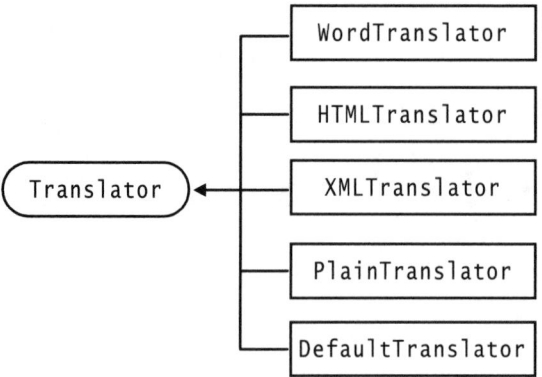

Figure 6-1   Translator framework

framework of Translator classes that handle different data types, as shown in Figure 6-1.

In this framework, Translator is a small interface, but each class that implements it can be very large. In fact, each translator might actually be a whole collection of classes. This means that the cost of loading a translator is large. Our example word processor uses a factory method to create the appropriate translator when a document is opened. This factory method is shown in Listing 6-1.

```
public static Translator getTranslator(String fileType) {
    if (fileType.equals("doc")) {
        return new WordTranslator();
    } else if (fileType.equals("html")) {
        return new HTMLTranslator();
    } else if (fileType.equals("txt")) {
        return new PlainTranslator();
    } else if (fileType.equals("xml")) {
        return new XMLTranslator();
    } else {
        return new DefaultTranslator();
    }
}
```

Listing 6-1   Simple factory method

In the process of tuning the word processor, it becomes evident that all of the translators are loaded before any document is opened—not just the particular translator needed for the document. Figure 6-2 shows a segment of the output displayed when the program is run with the -verbose flag on.

In this example, all of these classes are loaded because they are referenced from inside the same method. The JIT compiler of the runtime being used (Sun's

```
[Loaded .\WordTranslator.class]
[Loaded .\Translator.class]
[Loaded .\HTMLTranslator.class]
[Loaded .\PlainTranslator.class]
[Loaded .\XMLTranslator.class]
[Loaded .\DefaultTranslator.class]
```

Figure 6-2   Output from verbose class loading

Java 2 SDK v. 1.2 with the Symantec JIT) requires knowledge of all classes referenced by the method in order to compile it. To compile the method, all of the referenced classes are loaded. Since each translator is very large, several hundred kilobytes of memory might be consumed because these extra classes are loaded. Obviously, preventing them from being loaded would result in a significant savings in footprint. The next section discusses how to control eager loading in this situation.

6.1.1   Controlling Eager Loading

Reflection often gets a bad rap when it comes to performance tuning, and many programmers tend to avoid it out of habit. While reflection is slower than direct method dispatch, in some cases that doesn't matter. For example, when reflection is used to dispatch user events, such as button clicks, the amount of time required for reflective method dispatch is so small it's imperceptible. Even very low-end machines can perform more than 100 reflective method lookup and invoke operations per second.

In the word processor discussed in Section 6.1, reflection could be used to avoid loading all of the Translator implementations whenever one is needed. Listing 6-2 shows how the factory method can be rewritten using simple class reflection to avoid explicitly referencing any of the Translator implementations. Functionally, it's identical to the method shown in Listing 6-1.

```
public static Translator getTranslator(String fileType) {
    try {
        if (fileType.equals("doc")) {
            return (Translator)Class.forName(
                                "WordTranslator").newInstance();
        } else if (fileType.equals("html")) {
            return (Translator)Class.forName(
                                "HTMLTranslator").newInstance();
        } else if (fileType.equals("txt")) {
            return (Translator)Class.forName(
                                "PlainTranslator").newInstance();
```

```
        } else if (fileType.equals("xml")) {
            return (Translator)Class.forName(
                           "XMLTranslator").newInstance();
        } else {
            return new DefaultTranslator();
        }
    } catch (Exception e) {
        return new DefaultTranslator();
    }
}
```

Listing 6-2   Using reflection in a factory

In this version, there are no static references to the various `Translator` classes that the compiler can see directly. This prevents it from loading these classes early, even if it wants to. Instead, the classes are only loaded when the `Class.forName` method is called.

It's important to note that as runtimes improve, they'll prematurely load classes less often. There is already considerable variation in when classes are loaded from runtime to runtime. For example, the HotSpot compilers don't suffer from the specific problem described here, although many others do.

You shouldn't automatically use reflection everywhere in your program. In each case, you need to consider the benefits of controlling class loading against the costs of increased code complexity and reduced computational performance. This tactic is useful if large classes or a large number of classes are being loaded when you don't think they should be.

6.2   Reducing the Number of Classes

To illustrate several techniques for reducing class creation, let's look at the Java-Beans™ listener pattern. The JavaBeans model encourages the creation of many small classes, which can have a negative impact on footprint. However, there are many ways you can use the beans event mechanism, and some are lighter-weight than others.

JDK 1.1 introduced inner classes to the Java programming language. These powerful constructs enable developers to deal with the flexible event model introduced by the JavaBeans component architecture. Figure 6-3 shows a simple application written using the Swing `JButton` class, which is a bean. When a button is clicked, this program simply outputs a string to the console. In the following sections, several different versions of this program are used to illustrate the costs associated with different coding styles.

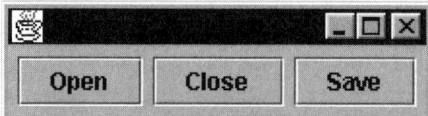

Figure 6-3 Simple GUI application

6.2.1 Simple Inner Classes

The code in Listing 6-3 uses inner-classes to attach listeners to a set of buttons. An inner class is created for each action that the user can perform, and an instance of each class is attached to one of the buttons. The `actionPerformed` method in the inner class then dispatches the event to the appropriate method in the enclosing class. (In a real program, the `open`, `close`, and `save` methods would obviously do more than print to the system console.)

```java
public class Listener1 extends JFrame {
    public Listener1() {
        JButton open = new JButton("Open");
        JButton close = new JButton("Close");
        JButton save = new JButton("Save");
        getContentPane().setLayout(new FlowLayout());
        getContentPane().add(open);
        getContentPane().add(close);
        getContentPane().add(save);
        open.addActionListener(new OpenAction());
        close.addActionListener(new CloseAction());
        save.addActionListener(new SaveAction());
        pack();
        setVisible(true);
    }
    protected void open() {
        System.out.println("Open a file");
    }
    protected void close() {
        System.out.println("Close a file");
    }
    protected void save() {
        System.out.println("Save a file");
    }

    class OpenAction implements ActionListener {
        public void actionPerformed(ActionEvent e) {
            open();
        }
    }
    class CloseAction implements ActionListener {
        public void actionPerformed(ActionEvent e) {
            close();
```

```
        }
    }

    class SaveAction implements ActionListener {
        public void actionPerformed(ActionEvent e) {
            save();
        }
    }

    public static void main(String[] args) {
        new Listener1();
    }
}
```

Listing 6-3   Simple GUI with inner classes

While this is a very clean, object-oriented solution, it is somewhat costly—
each inner class increases the program's RAM footprint. While the class files
generated for the inner classes are only a few hundred bytes each, they occupy
about 3K once loaded into RAM. (While the actual amount of RAM consumed is
implementation-dependent, 3K is typical for several runtimes.)

In this example, the inner classes only add about 10K to the program's RAM
footprint, which is negligible. A large, complex application, however, might need
100 listeners, which could consume several hundred kilobytes. If your application
falls into the latter category, it's probably worth optimizing to reduce the number
of classes that are loaded.

6.2.2   Collapsing the Listeners

One way to optimize the previous example so it consumes less RAM is to collapse
the listeners. The program could be written so that it functions identically with
only one listener, as shown in Listing 6-4.

```
class ButtonAction implements ActionListener {
        public void actionPerformed(ActionEvent e) {
            JButton b = (JButton)e.getSource();
            if ( b.getText().equals("Open") ) {
                open();
            } else if (b.getText().equals("Close")) {
                close();
            } else if (b.getText().equals("Save")) {
                save();
            }
        }
    }
```

Listing 6-4   Handling multiple events with a single listener

Listing 6-5 shows how this single listener class is used with each button. This implementation is functionally identical to the one shown in Listing 6-3. The advantage of this solution is that only one class is needed to handle the input from all of the buttons. Instead of three classes, only a single class needs to be loaded into memory.

```
ActionListener listener = new ButtonAction();
open.addActionListener(listener);
close.addActionListener(listener);
save.addActionListener(listener);
```

Listing 6-5   Adding the listeners

This solution is problematic, however. The primary problem is that it's more difficult to maintain. Whenever you see a *switch* structure like this in an object-oriented program, you know you're in trouble—it just doesn't scale well. If the program has 100 actions, you'd need 100 `if-then-else` clauses. Another problem with this approach is that the code is fragile. It's dependent on the names of the buttons, which are likely to change and might need to be localized. Although this optimization is an improvement in terms of footprint, the benefit isn't worth the impact on maintainability and stability.

6.2.3   Using Reflection

Another way to reduce the number of classes that are loaded to handle events is to use reflection. In the `Translator` example in Section 6.1.1, reflection was used to avoid loading classes. It can also be used to avoid creating classes at all. The code in Listing 6-6 shows a generic class that can be used to dispatch an action from any `ActionEvent` source to any zero-argument method on the target object.

```
class ReflectiveAction implements ActionListener {
String methodName;
Object target;
public ReflectiveAction(Object target, String methodName)
{
    this.target = target;
    this.methodName = methodName;
}
public void actionPerformed(ActionEvent e) {
    try {
        Class[] argTypes = {};
        Method method = target.getClass().getMethod(methodName,
                                                    argTypes);
        Object[] args = {};
        method.invoke(target, args);
```

```
        } catch (Exception ex) {
          ex.printStackTrace();
        }
    }
}
```

Listing 6-6   Generic `ActionListener`

To use this class, you create an instance of it and pass the constructor a target object and the name of the method to be called on the target. When an event arrives, `ReflectiveAction` looks up the method and calls it. Listing 6-7 shows how `ReflectiveAction` is used to add listeners to the buttons in a simple application.

```
open.addActionListener(new ReflectiveAction(this, "open"));
close.addActionListener(new ReflectiveAction(this, "close"));
save.addActionListener(new ReflectiveAction(this, "save"));
```

Listing 6-7   Adding `ReflectiveAction`s

Classes like `ReflectiveAction` are sometimes called *trampolines* because they spring you from one method to another. Trampolines are an attractive solution for a couple reasons.

- A single class can be used for any listeners of the same type.

- The code that results from their use is very clear.

Trampolines have some drawbacks, however. The biggest problem is that you lose compile-time type checking. If you mistype the name of a method, you'll wind up with a runtime error instead of a compile time error. There's also a minor performance hit because reflection is slower than direct method dispatch. However, the amount of time it takes to perform the lookup and call the method is so small that no user could perceive it. In many situations, using trampolines is a reasonable tactic for reducing footprint.

6.2.4   Using a Proxy

While trampoline classes like the one in Section 6.2.3 are useful in a wide range of situations, they don't work very well in highly dynamic environments such as builder tools. Such a tool would need to provide a trampoline class for every type of event that could be generated by any bean. Since the JavaBeans event model is extensible to an infinite number of event types, this isn't practical.

The Java 2 Standard Edition (J2SE) v. 1.3 introduces a new class called `java.lang.reflect.Proxy`. This class was designed to deal with just this situation. The `Proxy` class allows simple trampoline-style classes to be generated on the fly during runtime. This makes it possible to create a proxy builder that can generate a proxy for any listener type at runtime.

Note: `java.lang.reflect.Proxy` isn't recommended for use in your everyday programming. The code required is quite tricky and can be somewhat confusing. This tactic is best reserved for systems that demand maximum flexibility, such as JavaBeans assembly tools or other tools that allow users to configure actions. For such applications, `Proxy` is extremely powerful.

Listing 6-8 shows a class that builds dynamic proxy objects. This class implements the `java.lang.reflect.InvocationHandler` interface, which is a companion of the `Proxy` class. `InvocationHandler` defines a single method called `invoke`. This method allows you to specify how a particular call is to be routed through the proxy. This example simply ignores the arguments passed to the original function—no arguments are passed to the target object. A more full-featured implementation might pass along the arguments as well.

```
class DynamicProxy implements InvocationHandler {
   Object target;
   String methodName;
   public static Object makeProxy(Object target,
                                  String methodName,
                                  Class impl) {
      ClassLoader loader = target.getClass().getClassLoader();
      DynamicProxy handler = new DynamicProxy();
      handler.target = target;
      handler.methodName = methodName;
      // create a new proxy object
      // the object will implement the interface passed
      // into the impl parameter
      // it will dispatch all method calls to the proxy
      // to the target object via the invoke method below
      return Proxy.newProxyInstance(loader ,
                                    new Class[]{impl},
                                    handler);
   }
   public Object invoke(Object proxy, Method method,
                        Object[] args) {
      try {
         Object[] noArgs = {};
         Class[] argTypes = {};
```

```
            Method targetMethod = target.getClass().
                                        getMethod(methodName,
                                                   argTypes);
            return targetMethod.invoke(target, noArgs);
        } catch (Exception e ) {
            e.printStackTrace();
            return null;
        }
    }
}
```

Listing 6-8   Proxy generator

This `DynamicProxy` class provides a static method that creates a new proxy. You pass in the target for the proxy, the name of the method you want to call on the target, and the interface that the proxy will implement.

What goes on behind the scenes when you use a proxy is fairly complex. The first time you create a `Proxy` that implements a particular interface, a new class is created on the fly. For example, if the `Proxy` implements `ActionListener`, a class is created that is named something like `$ProxyActionListener`. You never directly interact with this class. Each time you call a method on the `Proxy`, it calls the `invoke` method of its `InvocationHandler`.

In the implementation of the `invoke` method, you redirect the method call however you see fit. In the `DynamicProxy` example, all method calls are redirected to a particular method on the specified target object. Listing 6-9 shows the code that creates the proxies and adds them to the buttons of our sample GUI application.

```
open.addActionListener(
(ActionListener)DynamicProxy.makeProxy(this, "open",
                                  ActionListener.class));
close.addActionListener(
(ActionListener)DynamicProxy.makeProxy(this, "close",
                                  ActionListener.class));
save.addActionListener(
(ActionListener)DynamicProxy.makeProxy(this, "save",
                                  ActionListener.class));
```

Listing 6-9   Adding the proxies

How does this tactic compare with using a trampoline? The runtime costs are similar. After a proxy is created for `ActionListener` the first time, subsequent proxies for the `ActionListener` don't cause a new class to be generated. Instead, you're handed a new instance of the previously created class. The advantage of using a proxy instead of a trampoline is that you won't have to create a new trampoline each time you need to use a new listener interface—it's created for you automatically. The disadvantage is that using a proxy is not as straightforward as using a trampoline.

6.2.5   Who Really Uses These Tactics?

Although some of these tactics for eliminating classes might seem a bit scary, similar techniques are being used successfully today—not only for JavaBeans listener classes, but in other situations as well. Reflection is used in several Swing classes to delay class loading. Early versions of Swing loaded many classes that were not needed in minimal applications. To solve this problem, techniques similar to those described in this chapter were used to delay the loading of those classes until they were actually needed.

   One example is the `UIDefaults` table, which contains much of the look-and-feel specific information for an interface. To avoid premature loading, it uses the `javax.swing.UIDefaults.ProxyLazyValue` class. The default `CellEditors` associated with the `javax.swing.JTable` class are loaded lazily using the same technique. These reflection-based solutions removed over 200 class loads for some of the applications we measured.

6.3   Running Multiple Programs

It is quite possible to run fairly sophisticated client-side Java programs on older hardware with as little as 32MB of RAM. However, running multiple Java applications at the same time poses more of a problem on lower-end hardware. Running multiple JVM instances on a single system can require a lot of memory, primarily because they share almost no state. For example, each JVM instance maintains private copies of all loaded classes. This includes classes your program's classes as well as any classes you load from the Java platform libraries.

   One solution to this problem is to run several programs inside the same JVM instance so that the programs can share loaded classes. This can result in a major reduction in the total memory used.

   The following sections use a simple office suite of programs to illustrate the costs of running multiple JVM instances. Sections 6.3.2 and 6.3.3 discuss a tactic you can use to reduce these costs.

6.3.1   The Office Suite

An office suite is a collection of programs used by businesses, such as a word processor and spreadsheet. As an example, we'll look at a simple office suite that consists of just two classes—one that implements a very basic spreadsheet, and another that implements a very basic word processor. Listing 6-10 shows the spreadsheet class. The word processor class is shown in Listing 6-11.

```
public class Spreadsheet {
    public static void main(String[] args) {
        JFrame f = new JFrame("Spreadsheet");
        JTable table = new JTable(20,5);
        JScrollPane scroller = new JScrollPane(table);
        f.setContentPane(scroller);
        f.setBounds(10,10,200,200);
        f.setVisible(true);
        f.addWindowListener(new WindowAdapter() {
            public void windowClosing(WindowEvent e) {
                System.exit(0);
            }});
    }
}
```

Listing 6-10   Simple spreadsheet

```
public class WordProcessor {
    public static void main(String[] args) {
        JFrame f = new JFrame("WordProcessor");
        JTextArea text = new JTextArea("Type Here");
        JScrollPane scroller = new JScrollPane(text);
        f.setContentPane(scroller);
        f.setBounds(10,10,200,200);
        f.setVisible(true);
        f.addWindowListener(new WindowAdapter() {
            public void windowClosing(WindowEvent e) {
                System.exit(0);
            }});
    }
}
```

Listing 6-11   Simple word processor

These programs can be run from the command line by entering java Spreadsheet or java WordProcessor. It is also possible to create simple batch files or shell scripts that execute these commands. This enables users on many operating systems to simply double-click the script files to run the programs.

The trouble starts when a user wants to run the spreadsheet and the word processor simultaneously, or run multiple copies of the same program. Memory requirements quickly start to spiral out of control. For example, the Windows NT Task Manager shown in Figure 6-4 shows the memory requirements for two spreadsheets and a word processor.

Image Name	PID	CPU	CPU Time	Mem Usage
sunwamdnt.exe	104	00	0:00:00	200 K
esserver.exe	108	00	0:00:00	108 K
CMD.EXE	111	00	0:00:00	280 K
mstask.exe	114	00	0:00:00	136 K
sens.exe	120	00	0:00:00	528 K
CMD.EXE	121	00	0:00:00	0 K
NDDEAGNT.EXE	127	00	0:00:00	148 K
EXPLORER.EXE	160	00	0:02:46	6260 K
LOADWC.EXE	167	00	0:00:00	108 K
DDHELP.EXE	211	00	0:00:00	408 K
WINZIP32.EXE	218	00	0:00:02	4496 K
CMD.EXE	238	00	0:00:01	32 K
TASKMGR.EXE	275	00	0:00:01	1196 K
CMD.EXE	310	00	0:00:00	1112 K
java.exe	319	00	0:00:02	8780 K
CMD.EXE	326	00	0:00:00	1064 K
java.exe	343	00	0:00:02	8816 K
CMD.EXE	348	00	0:00:00	1112 K
java.exe	351	00	0:00:01	8704 K

Figure 6-4   Running several applications

According to the Task Manager, each program is using nearly 9MB of RAM—about 26MB altogether! It's actually not quite as bad as it looks—some of the memory is taken up by native DLLs that are shared by all three programs. However, the shared space only accounts for 1 to 2MB per application—even taking the shared memory into account, together these applications are using 20 to 24MB. Obviously, this just isn't going to work on a system with limited RAM resources.

6.3.2   Running in the Same Virtual Machine

One way to reduce the amount of memory used is to run applications in the same instance of the virtual machine. It's fairly easy to write a program launcher that can run multiple programs inside the same JVM. Figure 6-5 shows a flow chart of how such a program launcher operates.

When the launcher is asked to start a program, it first checks to see if there is a JVM already running that is willing to run the program. If there is, the launcher asks that JVM to run the program and then exits. If there isn't, the launcher runs the program in its JVM instance and listens for requests from other launchers to run additional programs. As long as the first launcher continues to run, other launchers start up, pass their requests onto the older launcher, and then shut down. If the first launcher shuts down, the next time a launcher starts it will run the

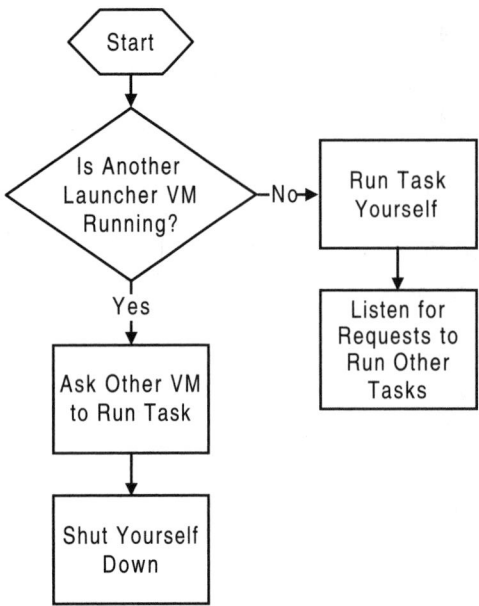

Figure 6-5   Flow chart for a simple launcher

requested program itself and begin handling requests from other launchers. Listing 6-12 shows the code for the Launcher class.

```
public class Launcher {
    static final int socketPort = 9876;

    public void launch(String className) {
        boolean launched = false;
        while (!launched) {
            System.out.println("Trying to launch:"+className);
            Socket s = findService();
            if (s != null) {
                System.out.println("found service");
                try {
                    OutputStream oStream = s.getOutputStream();
                    byte[] bytes = className.getBytes();
                    oStream.write(bytes.length);
                    oStream.write(bytes);
                    oStream.close();
                    launched = true;
                    System.out.println(className);
                } catch (IOException e) {
                    System.out.println("Couldn't talk to service");
                }
            } else {
                try {
```

```
                        System.out.println("Starting new service");
                        ServerSocket server = new ServerSocket(socketPort);
                        Launcher.go(className);
                        Thread listener = new ListenerThread(server);
                        listener.start();
                        launched = true;
                        System.out.println("started service listener");
                    } catch (IOException e) {
                        System.out.println("Socket contended, will try again");
                    }
                }
            }
        }
        protected Socket findService() {
            try {
                Socket s = new Socket(InetAddress.getLocalHost(), socketPort);
                return s;
            } catch (IOException e) {
                // couldn't find a service provider
                return null;
            }
        }
        public static void go(final String className) {
            System.out.println("running a " + className);
            Thread thread = new Thread() {
                public void run() {
                    try {
                        Class clazz = Class.forName(className);
                        Class[] argsTypes = {String[].class};
                        Object[] args = {new String[0]};
                        Method method = clazz.getMethod("main", argsTypes);
                        method.invoke(clazz, args);
                    } catch (Exception e) {
                        System.out.println("coudn't run the " + className);
                    }
                }
            }; // end thread sub-class
            thread.start();
        }
        public static void main(String[] args) {
            Launcher l = new Launcher();
            l.launch(args[0]);
        }
    }
```

Listing 6-12   Simple program launcher

To use the Launcher, you pass it the name of the class you want to run. The Launcher creates an instance of that class and calls its main method. Note that the Launcher also uses a class called ListenerThread. This class listens on a socket for requests to launch other programs.

Listing 6-13 contains the code for the `ListenerThread`. The `run` method of the `ListenerThread` class creates a `ServerSocket` and then runs in an infinite loop to serve launch requests.

```
public class ListenerThread extends Thread {
   ServerSocket server;

   public ListenerThread(ServerSocket socket) {
      this.server = socket;
   }

   public void run() {
      try {
         while (true) {
            System.out.println("about to wait");
            Socket socket = server.accept();
            System.out.println("opened socket from client");
            InputStream iStream = socket.getInputStream();
            int length = iStream.read();
            byte[] bytes = new byte[length];
            iStream.read(bytes);
            String className = new String(bytes);
            Launcher.go(className);
         }
      } catch (IOException e) {
         e.printStackTrace();
         System.out.println("Failed to start");
      }
   }
}
```

Listing 6-13   `ListenerThread`

Figure 6-6 shows the memory consumption from running the same three applications using the `Launcher`. In this case, only one JVM is running instead of three. The total memory consumption is less than 10MB, rather than the 20+MB required to run them in separate JVM instances. The great thing about using a launcher is that the savings continue to scale up as you run more applications.

6.3.3   A Better Launcher

There is a significant problem with the `Launcher` shown in Listing 6-12: Both the `Spreadsheet` and the `WordProcessor` classes call `System.exit(0)`. If the user closes any one of these programs, all of them will close.

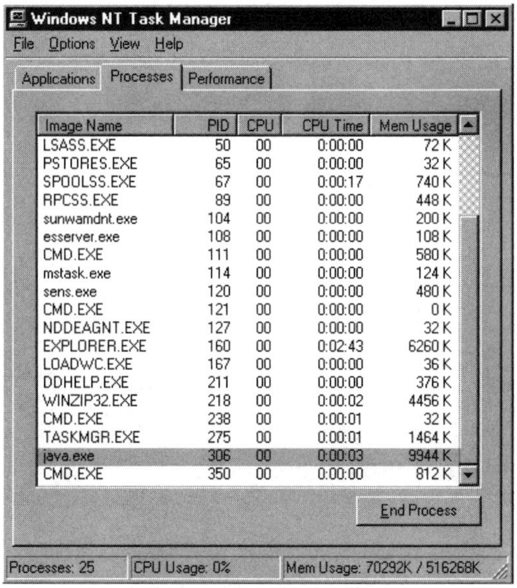

Image Name	PID	CPU	CPU Time	Mem Usage
LSASS.EXE	50	00	0:00:00	72 K
PSTORES.EXE	65	00	0:00:00	32 K
SPOOLSS.EXE	67	00	0:00:17	740 K
RPCSS.EXE	89	00	0:00:00	448 K
sunwamdnt.exe	104	00	0:00:00	200 K
esserver.exe	108	00	0:00:00	108 K
CMD.EXE	111	00	0:00:00	580 K
mstask.exe	114	00	0:00:00	124 K
sens.exe	120	00	0:00:00	480 K
CMD.EXE	121	00	0:00:00	0 K
NDDEAGNT.EXE	127	00	0:00:00	32 K
EXPLORER.EXE	160	00	0:02:43	6260 K
LOADWC.EXE	167	00	0:00:00	36 K
DDHELP.EXE	211	00	0:00:00	376 K
WINZIP32.EXE	218	00	0:00:02	4456 K
CMD.EXE	238	00	0:00:01	32 K
TASKMGR.EXE	275	00	0:00:01	1464 K
java.exe	306	00	0:00:03	9944 K
CMD.EXE	350	00	0:00:00	812 K

Figure 6-6 Running several applications with the launcher

Modifying the `Launcher` to work around this problem is fairly easy. You need to provide a mechanism through which a program can tell the `Launcher` it's closing, and track whether or not any programs are still running. The applications then needs to be modified to notify the `Launcher` when they quit instead of calling `System.exit`.

Adding a `programQuit` method to the `Launcher` class provides a way for programs to notify the `Launcher` that they are shutting down. This method is shown in Listing 6-14.

```
static int runningPrograms = 0;
public static void programQuit() {
   runningPrograms--;
   if (runningPrograms <= 0) {
      System.exit(0);
   }
}
```

Listing 6-14 Launcher `programQuit` method

You also need to add a `runningPrograms++` operation to the `Launcher.go` method so the `Launcher` can track how many programs are still running. When this number hits zero, the `Launcher` itself should shut down so that its resources are freed up for other uses.

In each application to be started through the `Launcher`, you also need to replace `System.exit` with

```
Launcher.programQuit();
e.getWindow().dispose();
```

You can download the complete source code for this and other examples from *http://java.sun.com/docs/books/performance/*.

> ## Key Points
>
> - The JVM sometimes loads classes before you think they are actually needed. Reflection techniques can be used to avoid this problem in some situations.
>
> - Creating a large number of small classes can increase a program's RAM footprint. There are several techniques for reducing the number of classes needed, without sacrificing good things like encapsulation and polymorphism.
>
> - Running multiple JVM instances can consume a lot of memory. You can reduce RAM requirements by running several programs inside the same JVM instance.

CHAPTER 7

Object Mutability:
Strings and Other Things

mu•ta•ble (myoóta bəl), adj. 1. liable or subject to change or alteration
2. given to changing; inconstant

—*Random House Webster's Dictionary*

WHILE most objects are mutable, some are not. For example, any bean that provides a setXXX method is mutable. Immutable objects can be used to define values or attributes that you don't want to be changed. For example, the class in Listing 7-1 could be used to define mathematical concepts such as pi or the speed of light in a vacuum. A simulation might set up these values in a method called bigBang; once they are set, the immutability of the MathematicalConstant class prevents them from being modified.

```
public class MathematicalConstant {
      private double value;
      public MathematicalConstant(double value) {
          this.value = value;
      }
      public double getValue() {
          return value;
      }
}
```
Listing 7-1   Immutable objects

Even though this example is somewhat academic, there are many cases where immutable objects are used in everyday programming. (The primary example of a class with immutable instances is String, which is discussed in Section 7.2.)

The choices you make when handling objects must take into account their mutability. With both mutable and immutable objects, it's possible to create numerous, useless, intermediate objects with seemingly benign usage. The allocation, initialization, and collection of these short-lived useless objects can cause major inefficiencies in your software, even when running on an advanced runtime such as the HotSpot VM.

7.1   Lots of Little Objects

The creation and destruction of objects is a performance bottleneck in most object-oriented languages. Many Smalltalk and C++ programmers have learned to be wary of allocating too many small objects. Developers using the Java programming language should share this concern. Creating many short-lived objects is a common performance bottleneck for software on the Java platform.

When you allocate a Java object with the keyword new, you are causing many things to happen. First, space is allocated on the heap for the object. Then, the class's constructor is called, and the class's fields are initialized. The object's status is then tracked so the garbage collector can determine if it should remove the object from the heap. (For a more detailed explanation of the lifecycle of an object, see Appendix A, The Truth About Garbage Collection.)

While there are obviously costs associated with creating objects, the situation is improving. Modern JVMs, such as the HotSpot VM, provide much faster object allocation and improved collection mechanisms. However, there will always be costs associated with object allocation.

It is important to note that while creating objects can be an issue, it isn't always a problem. Objects are a key part of the Java programming language. You can't write a program without creating objects. You just want to be cautious when the number of objects you're allocating becomes very high—for example, when allocating objects inside loops. As with other optimization decisions, you should let your profiler be your guide. If your profiling tools show that a large amount of time is being spent allocating a particular type of object, then you can use the techniques discussed in this chapter to reduce the number of objects used.

See Section 7.6 for more information about object allocation and collection in the HotSpot VM. For information about the technical details of HotSpot's GC system, see Section B.2.1 in Appendix B.

7.2   Handling String Objects

Text processing of one type or another is central to many types of software—Java servlets, for example, often perform a lot of String processing. The String class is typically used to represent text and offers many convenient methods that help with basic text processing tasks. For heavy-duty text processing, however, some uses of the String class can become major performance bottlenecks.

Most of the problems with using `String` stem from the fact that `String` objects are immutable. Once they've been created, they cannot be changed. Operations that might appear to modify `String` objects actually generate completely new ones.

This is one of the reasons that the `java.lang.StringBuffer` class exists. The `String` and `StringBuffer` classes are meant to be used together. This relationship even extends to the implementation of Java language compilers such as `javac`. For example, when `javac` encounters the code snippet

```
String xyz = "x" + y + "z";
```

It automatically transforms the code to

```
String xyz = new StringBuffer().append("x")
                               .append(y)
                               .append("z")
                               .toString();
```

This gives you an idea how `String` concatenation actually works. Note that two objects are created to perform the transformation: A new `StringBuffer` is created explicitly and a new `String` is returned from `toString`. Knowing this, the problem with concatenating a number of `String` objects as shown in Listing 7-2 becomes obvious.

```
String result = "";
for (int i=0; i < 20; i++) {
    result += getNextString();
}
```

Listing 7-2 Concatenating `String` objects

The `javac` compiler would automatically transform this to

```
String result = "";
for (int i=0; i < 20; i++) {
    result = new StringBuffer().append(result)
                               .append(getNextString())
                               .toString();
}
```

This code creates two objects every time through the loop—one `String-Buffer` and one `String` (via the call to `toString`). That's OK if you're only going to iterate over this loop a few times, but if you're going to be executing this code often you might want to handle the `String` objects differently. The code in Listing 7-3 produces the same results, but does not allocate any objects inside the loop. This approach is much more efficient.

```
String result = "";
StringBuffer buffer = new StringBuffer();
for (int i=0; i < 20; i++) {
    buffer.append(getNextString())
}
result = buffer.toString();
```

Listing 7-3   Concatenating `String` objects more efficiently

Another important fact to note is that the creation of extra `String` instances is not limited to occasions where the overloaded mathematical operators are used. There are several methods in the `String` class that generate new instances, including

- `concat`
- `replace`
- `substring`
- `trim`

Anytime you find yourself using one of these methods in a compute-intensive part of your code, you might want to consider using a `StringBuffer`.

7.3   Mutable Objects in AWT and Swing

The `java.awt` package defines several classes that encapsulate geometric information. These geometry classes are shown in Table 7-1.

Class	Description
`Point`	(x,y) location in space
`Dimension`	Component width and height
`Insets`	Representation of the borders of a container
`Rectangle`	Area in a coordinate space

Table 7-1   AWT Geometry Classes

The `java.awt.Component` and `java.awt.Container` classes define methods to access certain geometric information. These methods are shown in Listing 7-4.

```
public Point getLocation();
public void setLocation( Point loc);
```

```
public Dimension getSize();
public void setSize(Dimension size);
public Insets getInsets();
public void setInsets(Insets insets);
public Rectangle getBounds();
public void setBounds(Rectangle bounds);
```

Listing 7-4   Methods for accessing geometric information

This functionality illustrates the importance of decisions about mutability. What happens when the following code is executed?

```
Rectangle bounds = button.getBounds();
bounds.x += 10;
```

Is the component moved? The answer has to be no. AWT needs to prevent this type of operation to avoid inconsistencies. For example, when the `setBounds` method is called, AWT makes sure that the `Component` is marked *invalid*. This ensures that layout is performed properly. Similarly, many other types of actions and notifications occur when the geometry-related `set` methods are called. If you could directly modify a `Component` object's internal data structures, you could easily put it into an inconsistent state.

How does AWT prevent modification of the internal state of a `Component`? It returns a newly created `Rectangle` object every time `getBounds` is called. The actual internal representation of data in the `Component` remains private and is never passed outside the `Component` itself. For example, the code in Listing 7-5 actually creates four separate `Rectangle` objects:

```
int x = button.getBounds().x;
int y = button.getBounds().y;
int h = button.getBounds().height;
int w = button.getBounds().width;
```

Listing 7-5   `Component` mutability

Although several of these objects can be created without having a detectable effect on performance, creating large numbers of temporary objects can negatively impact performance. Profiling tools can help you determine whether or not temporary allocations are affecting your application's performance.

Small Objects in Swing

When the Swing team began performance tuning version 1.0 of Swing, profiling tools revealed that a large number of small objects were being created in performance-sensitive areas. For example, 12 temporary objects were allocated every time a cell in a JTable was painted. Similar problems were uncovered in many areas of the system. Eliminating a large percentage of these temporary allocations made many operations in Swing nearly twice as fast.

7.3.1   Eliminating Temporary Objects

So how do you eliminate temporary allocations while still maintaining solid data encapsulation? There are several possible solutions—which one is best depends on the particular circumstances.

Swing added methods to provide access to the information in the geometry objects directly, which eliminated the need to copy the objects. For example, the following methods were added to the JComponent class:

```
public int getX();
public int getY();
public int getHeight();
public int getWidth();
```

Because these methods return primitive types instead of objects, there is no need to worry about encapsulation being violated. With these methods, rather than writing

```
int width = comp.getSize().width; // allocates temp object
```

you can write

```
int width = comp.getWidth(); // no allocation
```

The primary drawback to this approach is that is complicates the public API of the class, which usually translates to

- Increased maintenance costs
- Increased documentation requirements
- A steeper API learning curve

Another problem with this solution is that it moves the responsibility for controlling mutability out of the object and into any object that wants to use it. In the previous Swing example, the Rectangle object's mutability is being controlled by JComponent. Any other class that wants to use Rectangle in a similar manner has to duplicate methods that already exist in JComponent.

For Swing, this was really the only solution—the Rectangle class has existed since JDK 1.0, and there were many reasons to reuse the existing class instead of creating one from scratch. However, if you don't have to deal with legacy classes, there are other solutions that can be very effective. Some of these are discussed in the next section.

7.4   Other Mutable Object Tactics

When you're designing new solutions rather than working with legacy code, you have more flexibility in how you choose to minimize temporary allocations. One tactic uses a concept similar to the const keyword defined in the C++ language.

7.4.1   Simulating const

If you've programmed in C++, you're already familiar with the concept of const objects. In C++, the const keyword allows you to specify that a particular object is to be treated as immutable. Any attempt to change a const object's state triggers a compiler error. Although the Java programming language doesn't provide a direct analog to const, it is fairly easy to structure your classes so that you can simulate it.

To demonstrate how simulating the behavior of const in a Java program can help minimize temporary allocations, we'll use two versions of a highly simplified physics simulation framework. The first implements the framework using traditional techniques similar to those used in AWT; the second uses the const technique. Both versions provide encapsulation of an object's internal data representation.

This simple physics simulation framework consists of two classes: Body and Location. A Body, as shown in Listing 7-6, has a mass and a location in space. A Location is a three-dimensional point that represents a body's position.

```
public class Body {
    private int mass = 10;
    private Location loc = new Location();

    public int getMass() {
        return mass;
    }
    public void setMass(int mass) {
        this.mass = mass;
```

```
    }
    public Location getLocation() {
        return new Location(loc.x, loc.y, loc.z);
    }
    public void move() {
        // we're just moving at random here
        // in a real sim we'd have forces and such
        loc.x += 1;
        loc.y += 2;
        loc.z += 3;
    }
}
```

Listing 7-6 Body

Listing 7-7 shows the Location class. Note that the getLocation method in the Body class returns a copy of the internally stored Location object—not a reference to the original. This is done to preserve encapsulation and prevents the Location fields from being modified by external code.

To analyze the performance of this small framework we can use a Simulation class. This class, shown in Listing 7-8, creates a large number of Body objects and performs various operations on them. This example simulation doesn't actually do any useful work, but it approximates the kind of work that might be performed in

const vs. final

The Java keyword final is often compared to the C++ const keyword, but they are in fact very different. Both const and final can be used to describe local variables, as well as object fields. When used in this context the two keywords are fairly similar. However, both const and final have other uses. The const keyword becomes very interesting when paired with the C++ reference mechanism. Together, they allow you to create const references to objects. For example, consider a C++ member function with the following prototype:

```
const Rectangle& getBounds();
```

This declares that the getBounds member function returns a const Rectangle reference. Although the Rectangle class can be constructed in such a way that objects of that type are normally mutable, anyone that calls this getBounds method will be unable to modify the state of the Rectangle that is returned. The Java language's final keyword has no similar functionality.

a real simulation. (A real simulation might simulate the effects of gravity or some other force.)

```java
public class Location {
    public int x;
    public int y;
    public int z;
    public Location() { }
    public Location(int x, int y, int z) {
        this.x = x;
        this.y = y;
        this.z = z;
    }
}
```

Listing 7-7   Location

```java
public class Simulation {

    static ArrayList bodies = new ArrayList();
    static final int NUM_BODIES = 200;
    static final int TIME_STEPS = 100000;

    public static void main(String[] args) {
        for (int i = 0; i < NUM_BODIES; i++) {
            bodies.add(new Body());
        }
        Stopwatch timer = new Stopwatch().start();
        for (int i = 0; i < TIME_STEPS ; i++) {
            doTimeStep(i);
        }
        timer.stop();
        System.out.println(timer.getElapsedTime());
    }

    public static void doTimeStep(int timeStep) {
        Iterator iter = bodies.iterator();
        while (iter.hasNext()) {
            Body body = (Body)iter.next();
            body.move();
            Location loc = body.getLocation();
            log(body, loc, timeStep);
        }
    }

    public static void log (Body body, Location loc, int time) {
        // log this info to somewhere
    }
}
```

Listing 7-8   A simple simulation

Method	Time
`Body.getLocation`	29.0%
`Simulation.doTimeStep`	20.7%
`Location.<init>`	11.7%
`Body.move`	7.9%
`java.util.AbstractList$Itr.hasNext`	6.3%

Table 7-2   Simulation Profiling Results

Running this simulation on our test configuration takes about 16 seconds. Using a profiling tool to analyze the simulation gives us a better understanding of where the time is spent.

The profiling results in Table 7-2 show that more than 40 percent of the time it takes to run the simulation is spent in two methods: `Body.getLocation` and the constructor for the `Location` class. Almost all of this overhead is related to copying the returned `Location` objects.

In a real simulation, more work would likely be done in `Body.move` or elsewhere in the `Simulation` class, so the percentages might be quite different. However, the overhead of copying the `Location` objects is still likely to be significant.

Since the profiling results indicate that a significant amount of time is being spent copying the `Location` objects, this is a good candidate for optimization. There are a number of ways you can improve performance in this situation without sacrificing encapsulation. One solution would be to do what Swing did for its geometry objects—add accessor methods to `Body`:

```
public int getX();
public int getY();
public int getZ();
```

This would improve performance, but there are drawbacks. For example, if the simulation framework were more full-featured there might be many internal objects. This could cause an explosion in the number of these accessor methods. For example, the interface of your `Body` class might have to change to include

```
public int getLocationX();
public int getLocationY();
public int getLocationZ();
public int getVelocityX();
public int getVelocityY();
public int getVelocityZ();
// and even more
```

Adding many methods like this to your public API can needlessly complicate your code. A better alternative would be to move the concept of mutability into the Location object. To do this, you can split the single Location class into two classes—one that is immutable and one that is mutable. Listing 7-9 shows the modified Location class.

Note that two things have changed from the original version in Listing 7-7. First, the fields of the class have been changed from public to protected. This means that these fields can only be accessed by subclasses of Location, or by other classes in the same package. Any client code outside the package that contains this class will be denied access to the fields. Since the fields cannot be directly accessed, get methods have been added for read-only access.

```
public class Location {
    protected int x;
    protected int y;
    protected int z;

    public Location() { }
    public Location(int x, int y, int z) {
        this.x = x;
        this.y = y;
        this.z = z;
    }

    public final int getX() { return x; }
    public final int getY() { return y; }
    public final int getZ() { return z; }
}
```

Listing 7-9   The new Location class

There are times when you need a mutable version of the Location class. The MutableLocation class, shown in Listing 7-10, is a subclass of Location. The main purpose of this subclass is to enable modification of the object's internal fields. This is done by adding set methods for each field.

```
public class MutableLocation extends Location{
    public MutableLocation() { }
    public MutableLocation(int x, int y, int z) {
        super(x,y,z);
    }
    public final void setX(int x) { this.x=x; }
    public final void setY(int y) { this.y=y; }
    public final void setZ(int z) { this.z=z; }
}
```

Listing 7-10   MutableLocation

Once you have the separate `Location` and `MutableLocation` classes, you can easily create an approximation of the C++ `const` facility. Internally, you store a `MutableLocation` object, but return it typed as a simple `Location` when you want to allow only read-only access. This is similar to returning a `const` reference in C++.

Listing 7-11 shows the changes that need to be made to the `Body` class to implement this behavior. In this version, the internally stored `Location` becomes a `MutableLocation`, and the `getLocation` method is changed to return a direct reference of the `loc` field, instead of a copy. Note that `getLocation` still returns a `Location`.

```
private MutableLocation loc = new MutableLocation();
public Location getLocation() {
        return loc;
}
```

Listing 7-11   Modifications to the `Body` class

If the following code is written in a package separate from the `Location` class, it will now cause compile-time errors:

```
Location loc = body.getLocation();
loc.x = 5; // field x is not accessible
loc.setX(5); // method setX not found in class Location
```

Be aware, however, that it is possible to cast the returned `Location` object to a `MutableLocation`. The following code will work and is quite dangerous.

```
Location loc = body.getLocation();
MutableLocation mLoc = (MutableLocation)loc;
mLoc.setX(5);
```

This is perfectly legal from the compiler's perspective and gives code in any package access to the internals of the `Location` object. By writing this code, however, you're explicitly asking to do dangerous things. Note that the C++ `const` keyword is subject to the same limitation. You can "cast away" `const`-ness, but do so at your own risk.

So, how does this new version of the `Location` code perform? Running the same simulation as before, the code executes in about 8 seconds—almost twice as fast as the previous version. These results are consistent with the profiling data we collected: The profiler indicated that almost half of the execution time was spent copying the `Location` objects.

7.5　Mutable Object Case Study

As part of the tuning efforts for J2SE v. 1.3, the java.math package was rewritten. The java.math package includes the classes BigDecimal and BigInteger. In older versions of J2SE, these classes were implemented mostly as C code. For version 1.3, they were ported entirely to use the Java language. (This project is discussed further in Section 9.3.2 on page 143.)

One of the goals of this project was to improve performance of these classes. BigInteger, much like String, is an immutable object. One of the key performance enhancements in the rewrite was to create a mutable version of BigInteger. A private class called MutableBigInteger was added to the package java.math, and although it isn't exposed as public API, it is used internally to speed up many operations. Mike McCloskey, the engineer at Sun who did most of the work on this project, had the following to say about it:

> The original BigInteger is well designed and easy to use, but it has a major performance drawback in its immutability. When you perform multistep operations such as gcd, modInverse, and modPow, you have to create a new immutable number every step you take. Some of these operations take hundreds or thousands of steps, so it was absolutely necessary to make a mutable multiprecision number so the calculations could be done in place. Then you save copying the bits around, initializations of new numbers, allocating memory for new numbers, garbage collection of temporary numbers, etc. That's why we use the MutableBigInteger class behind the scenes.[1]

7.6　Small Objects and the Modern JVM

One of the advertised advantages of the new generation of JVMs, such as the HotSpot VM, is that they radically improve the performance of allocation and collection of small objects. Benchmarks of the HotSpot VM show that this isn't just marketing; it really does deliver major improvements in small object handling. However, initialization and allocation costs do still exist and can be significant in many cases.

Table 7-3 shows results for the simple physics simulation benchmark from the previous section. The Classic VM column shows the execution times under the classic virtual machine implementation with the Symantec JIT. The HotSpot VM column shows the execution times under the HotSpot Client VM.

---

1. From an email exchange with Mike McCloskey.

Test	Classic VM	HotSpot VM
Copy return result	30,370 ms	16,260 ms
Don't copy return result	7,520 ms	8,510 ms

Table 7-3   Small objects under different JVM implementations

Interestingly, the penalty for creating a lot of small objects is much greater with the classic VM implementation. Under the classic implementation, the version of the benchmark that creates all the small objects is over four times slower than the version that does not.

Under the HotSpot Client VM, the penalty for creating all of the small objects is significantly reduced. However, there is still an obvious penalty. This means that creating large numbers of small objects can still be an issue, although not as critical an issue as it once was. (For more information about how the HotSpot VM implements garbage collection, see Memory Allocation and Garbage Collection on page 208.)

7.6.1   Object Pooling

The small object penalty is well known, and has led programmers using older JVMs to live in fear of small objects. Many articles have been published on the topic of object caching or object pooling. The Object Pool pattern uses some type of collection (such as a Vector, Hashtable, or raw array) to store free lists of objects. Generally, when the program starts, a number of objects are put into the pool. Then when the program needs a new instance of the object, it simply gets it from the free list. When the immediate use of this object is over, it is returned to the free list.

In the past, object pooling was often used successfully. However, with the new generation of JVM implementations that include advanced memory management systems, object pooling small objects is often counterproductive. The overhead of managing the object pool is often greater than the small object penalty. Pooling can also increase a program's memory footprint. The need for many of these small objects can often be avoided altogether by having control over object mutability. Pooling small objects is not a recommended tactic when you're working with the new generation of JVMs.

Although pooling small objects isn't recommended with newer JVM implementations, pooling large objects or objects that work with native resources can be useful. For example, large bitmaps or arrays are often good candidates for reuse. Classes like Thread or Graphics that require native resources are also often excellent candidates for caching. Large arrays are also good candidates due to the overhead of clearing all of the elements during initialization.

In short, when making decisions about caching or reusing objects, let your profiler be your guide. If you find that you're spending a lot of time creating a particular type of object, and you can't control the creation by manipulating its mutability, then you might want to consider pooling. Be aware, however, that pooling might actually hurt performance when used with small objects on new JVMs; be sure to benchmark so you can compare the different solutions.

7.7   Array Mutability

Just as with object mutability, you need to be aware of array mutability. In fact, mutability is often more important with arrays because they can be much larger than a typical object. The Java 2 collections classes introduce a new interface called `Iterator`. It is possible to use the `Iterator` interface in a fashion that provides you with immutable arrays. The following example is designed to show why such a construct is needed.

Listing 7-12 shows a fragment of a class that might be part of a program designed to help ship packages.

```
public class ShippingInfo {
   private static final String[] states = {
     "AK", "AZ", "CA", "DE", "NV", "NY"};
   // more stuff down here
}
```

Listing 7-12   Simple shipping class

The following code fragment could be used to iterate through the list of states and print them out.

```
for (int i = 0; i < ShippingInfo.states.length; i++) {
   System.out.println(ShippingInfo.states[i]);
}
```

This is easy enough, but using the `final` keyword with arrays can be tricky. The following code does not compile as you might expect.

```
ShippingInfo.states = new String[50];
```

It fails because you cannot assign values to `final` variables. The following code, however, is perfectly legal:

```
ShippingInfo.states[5] = "Java City";
```

This code replaces the entry for Nevada ("NV") with "Java City." Obviously, final arrays are not immutable, and passing them around can violate encapsulation. No syntax in the Java programming language provides a truly immutable array. This can lead to all kinds of inconsistencies. To avoid these problems, one solution is to make the following changes:

1. Make the array private.

2. Add a getStates method.

3. Return a copy of the states array from the getStates method.

This preserves encapsulation, but is likely to cause performance issues—especially if the array is large. The array in the shipping example represents the 50 states and contains a relatively small number of elements, but in another situation the array might contain thousands of elements. For example, the array might represent the part numbers for all of the parts in a new car. One way to avoid copying the array and still maintain encapsulation is to create an Iterator.

Listing 7-13 shows a custom class that implements the Iterator interface. This listing creates the Iterator as an inner class, which gives it access to the private states array. Note that the remove method, which is required by the Iterator interface, throws an UnsupportedOperationException. This is how the Collections Framework enables you to create a read-only Iterator.

```java
public class ShippingInfo {
    private static final String[] states = {
        "AK", "AZ", "CA", "DE", "NV", "NY"};

    public static Iterator getStates() {
        return new StateIterator();
    }

    public static class StateIterator implements Iterator {

        private int current = 0;
        /* from Iterator */
        public boolean hasNext() {
            return current < states.length;
        }

        /* from Iterator */
        public Object next() {
            return nextState();
        }

        /* from Iterator */
        public void remove() {
            throw new UnsupportedOperationException();
        }
```

```
      /* custom typesafe next */
      public String nextState() {
         if (current < states.length) {
            String state = states[current];
            current++;
            return state;
         } else {
            throw new NoSuchElementException();
         }
      }
   }
}
```

Listing 7-13   An `Iterator` as a read-only array

The following code snippet can be used to iterate through the array safely, without concern that it could be accidentally damaged.

```
Iterator iter = ShippingInfo.getStates();
while (iter.hasNext()) {
    System.out.println(iter.next());
}
```

Note that the Java 2 Collections Framework provides a great deal of infrastructure for creating read-only collections. For more information on this feature, see Section 8.4.10, Immutable Collections.

The tactic of adding a wrapper object to hide the mutability of an underlying structure isn't unique to arrays. In fact, you can use this general approach to hide the mutability of many types of structures. Doug Lea discusses this idea in Section 2.4.3 of his book *Concurrent Programming in Java.*[2]

---

2. Doug Lea, *Concurrent Programming in Java: Design Principles and Patterns, Second Edition,* pp. 132–135. Addison-Wesley, 1999. Chapter 2 provides a good introduction to some of the problems associated with encapsulation in a multithreaded environment and is well worth reading.

Key Points

- Encapsulation is important, and an object's mutability has major implications for how an object's internal data representation should be protected.

- Creating many objects has an impact on performance, even with advanced runtime systems such as the HotSpot VM.

- String objects are immutable, thus many string operations create new String objects.

- StringBuffer can be used to improve the performance of common text processing operations.

- AWT, Swing and other libraries return a new copy of an object each time an accessor method is called. This can lead to the creation of many small objects.

- There are tactics you can use to avoid copying mutable objects while still preserving encapsulation.

- While there is no syntax in the Java programming language for creating immutable arrays, you can use the Iterator class to simulate them.

CHAPTER 8

Algorithms and Data Structures

UNDERSTANDING how to choose the best algorithm or data structure for a particular task is one of the keys to writing high-performance software. If you start with the wrong algorithm, all the micro-level tuning in the world won't produce optimal results.

This chapter discusses how to select and evaluate algorithms and data structures and addresses how these choices can affect the performance of your Java programs. Section 8.4 provides an introduction to the Java 2 Collections Framework, which contains a variety of high-performance data structures and algorithms that you can use.

A full introduction to algorithms and data structures would be an entire book by itself—in fact, the study of algorithms and data structures has been the subject of many books and papers. If you'd like to read more on this subject, see Section 8.6 for some good references.

8.1   Selecting Algorithms

When you choose an algorithm, there are always trade-offs involved. An algorithm might be the fastest solution for one type of data, but perform significantly slower for others. For example, there is no single sorting algorithm that is optimal in all situations. You have to consider how the algorithm is going to be used and select the solution that provides the best results most often.

For example, let's look at two different ways to calculate the sum of all integers that fall within a specified range. One solution is to simply build a loop around an addition statement, as shown in Listing 8-1.

```
public class SimpleSummer {
    public long sum(int start, int stop){
        long acc = 0;
        for(int i=start;i<=stop;i++){
            acc += i;
        return acc;
    }
}
```

Listing 8-1   Simple sum computer

As long as the number of integers to be summed is small, this simple algorithm works just fine. However, as the number of integers to be summed increases, the amount of time required to execute this algorithm grows linearly. This is what's known as an *order-N function*, which is abbreviated *O(n)* in big-oh notation.[1]

If your program needed this number-summing functionality and profiling showed that this function was a hot spot, you would probably want to speed it up. Your first inclination might be to tune the implementation of the algorithm. While in some cases tuning the existing algorithm might help, this implementation is pretty simple and there isn't much you can do. A more effective approach would be to consider other solutions.

For example, there is another way to sum a series of integers. The sum of any series of integers between zero and n, inclusive, can be calculated with the formula $(n(n+1))/2$. To calculate the sum of the series between n and m, inclusive, you can use the technique shown in Listing 8-2.

```
public class FormulaicSummer {
    public long sum(int start, int stop){
        int bigseries = stop*(stop+1)/2;
        start--; // so result is inclusive of start
        int littleseries = start*(start+1)/2;
        return bigseries-littleseries;
    }
}
```

Listing 8-2   Smarter sum computer

This method returns the result for any `start` and `stop` values in a fixed amount of time, regardless of how many numbers are summed. This is called an *order-1* or constant-time function, commonly abbreviated *O(1)*.

---

1. For more information about big-oh notation, see Andrew Binstock and John Rex, *Practical Algorithms for Programmers*, p. 2. Addison-Wesley, 1995.

8.1.1   Comparing Algorithms

Once you have alternate solutions like our two sum computers, you can compare them and choose the one that performs best for your program. The easiest way to compare the algorithms is to write a benchmark.

Listing 8-3 shows the code for a micro-benchmark that compares the two summing algorithms. (In practice, it's best to test alternative algorithms under different situations on multiple pieces of data—micro-benchmarks don't always show real-world results. For our simple example, however, this micro-benchmark is sufficient.)

```
public static void main(String args[]) {
   System.out.println("Sum integers between 13 and 1000");
   System.out.println("SimpleSummer:");
   long acc;
   SimpleSummer ss = new SimpleSummer();
   long time = System.currentTimeMillis();
   for (int i=0;i<5000;i++)
      acc = ss.sum(13,1000);
   long time2 = System.currentTimeMillis();
   System.out.println("Took "+(time2-time)+" ms.");
   System.out.println("FormulaicSummer:");
   FormulaicSummer fs = new FormulaicSummer();
   time = System.currentTimeMillis();
   for (int i=0;i<5000;i++)
      acc = fs.sum(13,1000);
   time2 = System.currentTimeMillis();
   System.out.println("Took "+(time2-time)+" ms.");
   }
```

Listing 8-3   Micro-benchmark

The results of this benchmark show that the constant-time algorithm is much faster than the linear algorithm for the specified inputs—the *order-N* algorithm was 65 times slower on our test configuration. As this example illustrates, switching to a smarter algorithm can lead to significant performance improvements that might be impossible to realize through tuning alone.

Order-N algorithms are not always a bad choice—in fact, they often provide the best solution. A more common problem is algorithms that have performance characteristics *worse* than order-N, where the time required to execute the algorithm increases nonlinearly as the amount of data increases. Algorithms that exhibit such *super-linear* performance characteristics, such as $O(n^2)$ algorithms, are a common cause of performance degradation and are a leading cause of poor scalability.

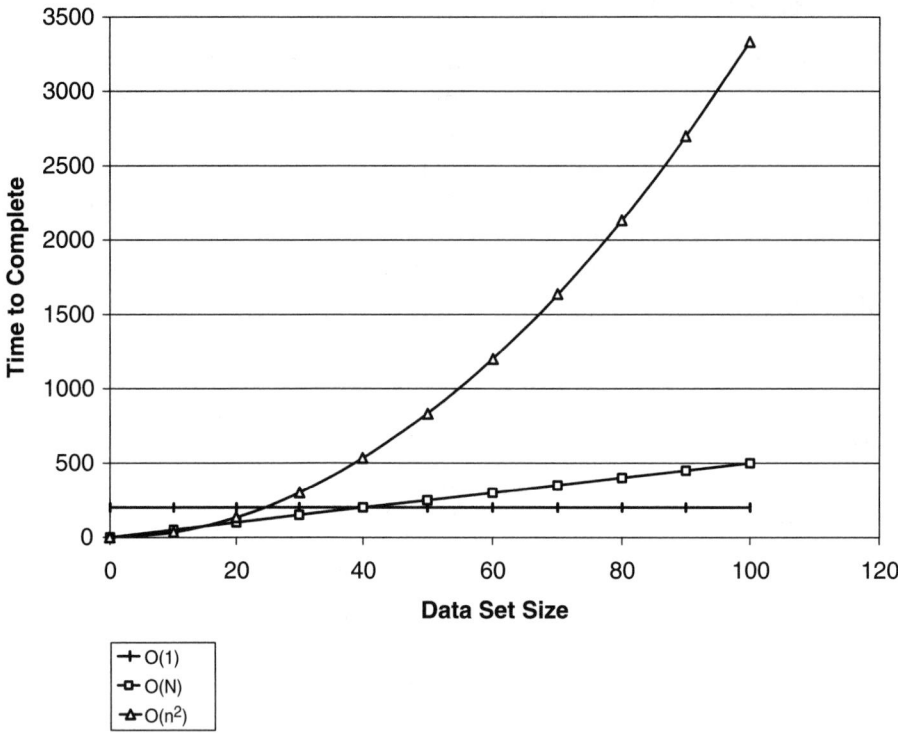

Figure 8-1 Comparison of algorithm performance

Figure 8-1 shows performance results for three theoretical algorithms that produce identical results. As you can see, it is possible for an order-N or N-squared algorithm to perform better than a constant-time algorithm on low numbers of data points. If you know you're only going be working with small amounts of data, the constant-time algorithm might be a poor choice. Similarly, if you're working with large or unpredictable amounts of data, using the N-squared algorithm could lead to significant performance problems.

8.1.2 Achieving Elegance

Computer scientists and software engineers sometimes discuss the *elegance* of a piece of code. Elegant code, like good art, is a bit hard to define. However, an elegant solution is generally one that approaches the problem in a way that is minimally complex and maximally suited to the particular problem being solved. As a result, elegant code is almost always fast code. One rule of thumb is that an elegant solution is one that you wouldn't mind calculating by hand.

In contrast, solutions such as the iterative loop in Listing 8-1 are referred to as *brute-force* solutions. Such solutions only work because computers can do repetitive tasks very quickly. When you find yourself tuning a brute-force solution to remove a bottleneck, consider whether there is a more elegant way to approach the problem. It's very possible that no amount of micro-tuning will significantly improve performance, while changing the algorithm could eliminate the bottleneck entirely.

8.1.3   Considering the Problem Space

When deciding what algorithm to use, it is important to take the *problem space* into account. The problem space is the set of problems with which an algorithm will be presented. You can often achieve a more efficient solution by constraining the algorithm to handle only the defined problem space instead of using a more general algorithm. In short, what your program *doesn't* do is often as important as what it does.

To illustrate this point, let's look at a common problem in graphics programming: drawing lines. The grid drawing framework shown in Listing 8-4 fills a canvas with a grid of lines. Line drawing is implemented as a general framework based on a LineDrawer interface so we can easily compare the performance of different line drawing algorithms.

```
// Grid container
public class GridTest extends JFrame {
    GridCanvas myCanvas;
    TextField status;

    public GridTest(LineDrawer ld) {
        super(ld.getClass().toString());
        getContentPane().setLayout(new BorderLayout());
        setSize(500,500);
        status = new TextField("TESTING: Do not disturb!");
        myCanvas = new GridCanvas(ld,status);
        getContentPane().add(myCanvas,BorderLayout.CENTER);
        getContentPane().add(status,BorderLayout.SOUTH);
        setDefaultCloseOperation(DISPOSE_ON_CLOSE);
        show();
        myCanvas.test();
    }

    public void closetest() {
        dispose();
    }

}
```

```
// Grid surface with timing code
public class GridCanvas extends JComponent {
    LineDrawer ld;
    TextField status;
    static long acc=0;
    BufferedImage bi;

    public GridCanvas(LineDrawer ld, TextField status){
        this.ld = ld;
        this.status = status;
    }

    public void test(){
        Rectangle r = getBounds();
        bi = new BufferedImage(r.width,
                               r.height,
                               BufferedImage.TYPE_INT_RGB);
        Stopwatch watch = new Stopwatch();
        for (int j=0;j<10;j++) { // do 10 tiems for stability
            watch.reset().start();
            for (int i =0; i< (r.height-1)/2; i++) {
                ld.drawLine(bi,0,i*2,r.width-1,i*2);
            }
            for (int  i=0; i<(r.width-1)/2;i++) {
                ld.drawLine(bi,i*2,0,i*2,r.height-1);
            }
            watch.stop();
            acc += watch.getElapsedTime();
        }
        status.setText("Time (ms) to do grid = "+(acc/10));
        repaint();
    }

    public void paint(Graphics g) {
        g.drawImage(bi,0,0,this);
    }
}


// The LineDrawer interface
public interface LineDrawer {
        public void drawLine(BufferedImage i,int x0, int
                                      y0, int x1, int y1);
}
```

Listing 8-4   Grid test framework

An object that implements the LineDrawer interface is passed to the framework to draw the lines into the BufferedImage. Listing 8-5 shows a concrete implementation of LineDrawer that's based on Bresenham's algorithm, a well-known, efficient algorithm for general line drawing.

```
public class BasicBresenham implements LineDrawer {
    public void drawLine(BufferedImage bi,
                         int x0, int y0,
                         int x1, int y1) {
        int dx,dy;
        int temp;
        // reduce to half the octant cases by always
        // drawing + in y
        if (y0>y1) {
            temp = y0;
            y0 = y1;
            y1 = temp;
            temp = x0;
            x0 = x1;
            x1 = temp;
        }
        dx = x1-x0;
        dy = y1-y0;
        if (dx>0) {
            if (dx>dy) {
                octant0(bi,x0,y0,dx,dy,1);
            } else {
                octant1(bi,x0,y0,dx,dy,1);
            }
        } else {
            dx = -dx;
            if (dx>dy) {
                octant0(bi,x0,y0,dx,dy,-1);
            } else {
                octant1(bi,x0,y0,dx,dy,-1);
            }
        }
    }
    private void octant0(BufferedImage bi,
                         int x0, int y0,
                         int dx, int dy,
                         int xdirection){
        int DeltaYx2;
        int DeltaYx2MinusDeltaXx2;
        int ErrorTerm;
        int pix = 0xffffffff;
        // set up initial error term and drawing values
        DeltaYx2 = dy*2;
        DeltaYx2MinusDeltaXx2 = DeltaYx2 - (dx*2);
        ErrorTerm = DeltaYx2 - dx;
        // draw loop
        bi.setRGB(x0,y0,pix); // draws a single point
        while ( dx-- > 0) {
        // check if we need to advance y
            if (ErrorTerm >=0) {
                // advance Y and reset ErrorTerm
                y0++;
                ErrorTerm += DeltaYx2MinusDeltaXx2;
            } else {
```

```
                // add error to ErrorTerm
                ErrorTerm += DeltaYx2;
            }
            x0 += xdirection;
            bi.setRGB(x0,y0,pix);
        }
    }
    private void octant1(BufferedImage bi,
                         int x0, int y0,
                         int dx, int dy,
                         int xdirection){
        int DeltaXx2;
        int DeltaXx2MinusDeltaYx2;
        int ErrorTerm;
        int pix = 0xffffffff;
        // set up initial error term and drawing values
        DeltaXx2 = dx * 2;
        DeltaXx2MinusDeltaYx2 = DeltaXx2 - (dy*2);
        ErrorTerm = DeltaXx2- dy;
        // draw loop
        bi.setRGB(x0,y0,pix);
        while ( dy-- > 0) {
        // check if we need to advance x
            if (ErrorTerm >= 0) {
                // advance X and reset ErrorTerm
                x0 += xdirection;
                ErrorTerm += DeltaXx2MinusDeltaYx2;
            } else {
                // add to ErrorTerm
                ErrorTerm += DeltaXx2;
            }
            y0++;
            bi.setRGB(x0,y0,pix);
        }
    }
}
```

Listing 8-5   General-purpose line drawing algorithm

Bresenham's[2] is a very efficient, general-purpose algorithm for drawing lines. Switching to a different general-purpose line drawing algorithm probably wouldn't gain us anything. However, if you carefully consider this application's problem domain, it is possible to find a better solution. Bresenham's is designed to draw lines of any arbitrary slope, but this application draws a grid that consists of lines that are either completely horizontal or completely vertical. Listing 8-6 shows a line drawer that uses this information about the problem space to provide a simpler solution.

---

2. For more information about Bresenham's algorithm, see Michael Abrash, *Graphics Programming Black Book, Special Edition,* pp. 657–678. The Coriolis Group, 1997.

To compare the two algorithms, we'll use the simple benchmark wrapper in Listing 8-7, which can invoke `GridTest` with either line drawing solution.

```
public class FlatLiner implements LineDrawer {
 static int pix = 0xffffffff;
   static int[] pixa = new int[0];
   static int pixasz = 0;
  public void drawLine(BufferedImage bi, int x0, int y0, int x1, int y1){
      if (x0 == x1) {
          int h = (y1-y0);
          if (h < 0) h = 0-h;
          h++;
          if (h>pixasz) {
              pixasz = h;
              pixa = new int[h];
              for (int i=0;i<pixasz;i++) pixa[i] = 0xffffffff;
          }
          bi.setRGB(x0,y0,1,h,pixa,0,1);
      } else if (y0 == y1) {
          int w = x1-x0;
          if (w < 0) w = 0-w;
          w++;
          if (w>pixasz) {
              pixasz = w;
              pixa = new int[w];
              for (int i=0;i<pixasz;i++) pixa[i] = 0xffffffff;
          }
          bi.setRGB(x0,y0,w,1,pixa,0,pixasz);
      } else {
          throw (new RuntimeException("FlatLiner called on "
                                      + "non-flat line"));
      }
    }
  }
}
```

Listing 8-6 Special-purpose line drawing algorithm

```
public class GridBenchmark {

  public static void main(String args[]) {
      if (Array.getLength(args) < 1) {
          System.out.println("usage: GridBenchmark b|f");
          System.exit(0);
      }
      if ((args[0].startsWith("b")) ||
          (args[0].startsWith("B"))) {
          new GridTest(new BasicBreshenham());
      } else {
          new GridTest(new FlatLiner());
      }
    }
  }
}
```

Listing 8-7 Benchmark wrapper for grid drawing

On our test configuration, the FlatLiner implementation ran approximately 25 percent faster than the BasicBresenham implementation. This result is typical—special-purpose algorithms usually run faster than general-purpose algorithms. When selecting an algorithm, consider your problem space and try constraining your solution to just the necessary operations.

Keep in mind that alternate solutions aren't necessarily mutually exclusive—in many cases it's possible to dynamically select the best algorithm. For example, the FlatLiner and BasicBresenham implementations can be combined by invoking Bresenham's algorithm inside FlatLiner. Instead of throwing an exception for lines with undefined slopes or slopes other than 0, simply insert the code from the BasicBresenham implementation. This results in a general-purpose solution that is just as fast as FlatLiner for simple grids and almost as fast as the general-purpose Bresenham's for all other lines. The cost of the two extra if-statements is negligible. This tactic of testing for easy-to-solve subcases is a mainstay of high-performance programming.

8.2   Using Recursive Algorithms

Recursion is a handy programming tool—many algorithms can be expressed naturally in recursive form. Problems that are complex or extremely difficult to solve using linear techniques often have simple recursive solutions. Although conventional wisdom often advocates avoiding recursion, it can offer the best solution to some problems. Not all programming languages support recursion, but the Java programming language does.

Recursive algorithms usually take the form shown in Listing 8-8, where the algorithm repeatedly calls itself, simplifying the problem at each iteration.

```
Solveit(problem) {
    if (problem is trivial) {
        return result;
    } else {
        simplify problem;
        return SolveIt(simplified problem);
    }
}
```

Listing 8-8   Pseudocode for recursion

For example, Listing 8-9 shows a simple, recursive algorithm for reversing the letters in a String.

```
public class TrivialApplication {
    public static void main(String args[]) {
        System.out.println( reverseString("Hello World!"));
    }
    static public String reverseString(String s){
        if (s.length() <= 1)
            return s;
        else {
            char c = s.charAt(0);
            eturn reverseString(s.substring(1))+c;
        }
    }
}
```

Listing 8-9   Recursive string reverser

If recursion is so useful, why would you want to avoid it? From a performance perspective, there are two potential problems with using recursion: memory consumption and the overhead of successive function calls.

Each successive call to a function creates a new stack frame. If the function is called too many times, the program could potentially run out of memory. For example, passing in a very long string to the `reverseString` method in Listing 8-9, might cause a `StackOverflowError` to be thrown.

The performance of a recursive algorithm can be affected by the overhead of the successive function calls. In languages like C++, the overhead is so great that recoding a naturally recursive algorithm using nonrecursive techniques is almost always a performance win.

In the Java language, the overhead of successive function calls can be less of an issue. For example, let's look at both recursive and nonrecursive implementations of the Towers of Hanoi problem.[3] Listing 8-10 shows the recursive solution.

```
public static void Towers(int numDisks,
                          char src, char dest, char temp){
    if (numDisks == 1) {
        System.out.println("Move top disk from pole "+
                            src+" to pole "+dest);
    } else {
        Towers(numDisks-1,src,temp,dest);
        Towers(1,src,dest,temp);
        Towers(numDisks-1,temp,dest,src);
    }
}
```

Listing 8-10   Recursive Towers of Hanoi

---

3. For more information about the Towers of Hanoi problem, see *http://www.pangea.ca/kolar/ javascript/Hanoi/HTonWEBE.html.*

The nonrecursive solution is much more complex. To implement the solution as a linear routine, shown in Listing 8-11, you have to create and manage your own stack and ensure that items are pushed in the right order. Despite the increase in complexity, conventional wisdom is that this version should be faster.

```java
public static void LinearTowers(int orig_numDisks,
                                char orig_src, char orig_dest,
                                char orig_temp){
    int numDisksStack[] = new int[100];
    char srcStack[] = new char[100];
    char destStack[] = new char[100];
    char tempStack[] = new char[100];
    int stacktop = 0;
    numDisksStack[0] = orig_numDisks;
    srcStack[0] = orig_src;
    destStack[0] = orig_dest;
    tempStack[0] = orig_temp;
    stacktop++;
    while (stacktop>0) { // this is the same as having
                         // call frames on the system stack
        stacktop--; // pop current off stack
        int numDisks = numDisksStack[stacktop];
        char src = srcStack[stacktop];
        char dest = destStack[stacktop];
        char temp = tempStack[stacktop];
        if (numDisks == 1) {
            System.out.println("Move top disk from pole "
                               + src + "to pole " + dest);
        } else {
            /* do this after the other two */
            /* Towers(numDisks-1,temp,dest,src); */
            numDisksStack[stacktop] = numDisks -1;
            srcStack[stacktop] = temp;
            destStack[stacktop] = dest;
            tempStack[stacktop++] = src;
            /* do this after the first */
            /* Towers(1,src,dest,temp); */
            numDisksStack[stacktop] =1;
            srcStack[stacktop] = src;
            destStack[stacktop] = dest;
            tempStack[stacktop++] = temp;
            /* do this first */
            /* Towers(numDisks-1,src,temp,dest); */
            numDisksStack[stacktop] = numDisks -1;
            srcStack[stacktop] = src;
            destStack[stacktop] = temp;
            tempStack[stacktop++] = dest;}
    }
}
```

Listing 8-11   Nonrecursive Towers of Hanoi

To compare the two algorithms, we'll use the program shown in Listing 8-12. Note that the `println` call in each implementation is actually much slower than the calculation and needs to be removed so we can get a realistic measurement of the calculation speeds.

```
public static void main(String args[]) {
    Stopwatch watch = new Stopwatch();
    watch.reset().start();
    Towers(25,'A','B','C');
    watch.stop();
    System.out.println("Time to solve recursively = "+
                        watch.getElapsedTime());
    watch.reset().start();
    LinearTowers(25,'A','B','C');
    watch.stop();
    System.out.println("Time to solve lineraly = "+
                        watch.getElapsedTime());
}
```

Listing 8-12   Timing harness for the Towers of Hanoi

As it turns out, the recursive version runs about 15 percent faster under our test configuration. Why isn't the nonrecursive version faster, as it probably would be in a C++ program?

Many variables might be affecting the performance of these algorithms, but one possible reason that the linear version is slower is that the JVM performs bounds checking on array access. This means that every time the linear version of the algorithm manipulates its artificial stacks, the JVM has to check the array index to make sure it is valid. In this case, these bounds checks seem to cost more than invoking a static method.

This example illustrates the importance of measuring performance before you begin optimizing your code. Unless you run a benchmark to compare the two algorithms, you might be inclined to linearize this method on the assumption that it would improve performance. In this case, that would just lead to slower, less maintainable code.

8.3   Beyond Simple Algorithms

When considering algorithms, programmers often focus on the merits of heavily studied algorithms, such as different sorting and hashing algorithms. While this is important, keep in mind that algorithms aren't just neat, well-defined solutions for standard tasks. Algorithms pervade your code and have a major impact on the performance of your software.

A real-life example of this was found in the `JComboBox` component in early versions of the Swing toolkit. Bugs were filed against `JComboBox`, noting that it took an extremely long time to add items to a `JComboBox` object's drop-down list. Further testing showed that performance was fine for small numbers of items, but as the number of items grew, the time it took to add them grew exponentially. It turned out that adding items to a `JComboBox` exhibited $O(n^2)$ behavior. In other words, if it took 100 milliseconds to add 10 items, it might take 10 seconds to add 100 items. For large numbers of items, this behavior obviously wasn't acceptable.

As it turned out, this N-squared behavior wasn't caused by the implementation of a single method. It was the result of interactions between several classes involved in the operation of `JComboBox`. Once the problem was identified, it was possible to rewrite selected classes to make the behavior more closely resemble a $O(n)$ algorithm. These changes significantly reduced the start-up times of many applications. Understanding this problem also made it possible to document that there were different ways to use `JComboBox`. One technique allows items to be added in a constant-time fashion, which further improved the performance of many applications. (For more information about `JComboBox` performance issues, see Chapter 10, Swing Models and Renderers.)

8.4 Selecting Data Structures

Selecting the appropriate data structure for your task is often just as important as selecting the algorithm. Just as with algorithms, there are trade-offs that need to be weighed when selecting a data structure—no single data structure is appropriate for all situations. This section discusses the data structures supplied with the Java 2 platform and some of the trade-offs to consider when using them.

8.4.1 Java 2 Collections

The Java platform has always provided a few basic data structures in the form of the `java.util.Vector` and `java.util.Hashtable` classes. Although they have been used successfully by thousands of developers, these classes have a number of performance-related problems. The Java 2 platform introduced an expanded set of data structures known as the *Collections Framework*. The classes in this framework address a number of the shortcomings of the `Vector` and `Hashtable` classes and add some high-performance algorithms for tasks such as sorting.

What Is a Collection?
A collection is an object that groups multiple elements into a single unit. Collections are used to store, retrieve, and manipulate data. They are also used to

transmit data from one method to another. Collections typically represent data items that form a natural group such as

- A poker hand: a collection of cards
- A mail folder: a collection of letters
- A telephone directory: a collection of name-to-phone-number mappings

The Collections Framework is a unified architecture for representing and manipulating collections that reduces programming effort while increasing performance. The framework is designed to

- Enable collection data to be manipulated independent of its representation
- Facilitate interoperability between unrelated APIs
- Reduce effort in designing and learning new APIs
- Foster software reuse

By providing high-performance, high-quality implementations of useful data structures and algorithms, the Collections Framework helps you improve the quality and performance of your software. The implementations of each interface are interchangeable, which makes it possible to tune a program by simply switching collection implementations. These ready-to-use data structures free you from the drudgery of writing custom data structures, leaving you with more time to devote to improving the quality and performance of the rest of your program.

8.4.2   The Collection Interfaces

The Collections Framework is based on six collection interfaces. The framework provides implementations of each these interfaces and algorithms to manipulate them. Figure 8-2 shows the hierarchy of interfaces and classes that make up the core of the framework.

The interfaces in the Collections Framework define the types of data structures the framework provides. Each type of data structure is best suited for a particular type of task. Understanding the purpose of each of these data structures will enable you to select the best data structure for a task. For some of the interfaces, the framework provides multiple, concrete implementations. To achieve optimal speed and memory utilization, you need to use the implementation best suited to the task. The purpose of each interface and the trade-offs involved in using the various implementations are discussed in the following sections.

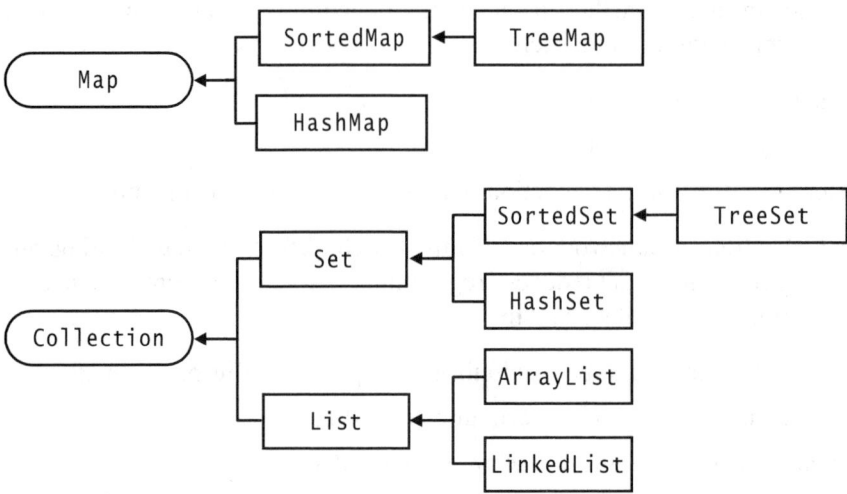

Figure 8-2   Collections Framework class hierarchy

8.4.3   `Collection` Interface

The `Collection` interface is the foundation of the Collections Framework; it defines the basic functionality implemented by all collections. A `Collection` represents a group of objects, which are known as the collection's elements. Listing 8-13 shows the methods defined by the `Collection` interface.

```
public interface Collection {
    int        size();
    boolean    isEmpty();
    boolean    contains(Object o);
    Iterator   iterator();
    Object[]   toArray();
    Object[]   toArray(Object a[]);
    boolean    add(Object o);
    boolean    remove(Object o);
    boolean    containsAll(Collection c);
    boolean    addAll(Collection c);
    boolean    removeAll(Collection c);
    boolean    retainAll(Collection c);
    void       clear();
    boolean    equals(Object o);
    int        hashCode();
}
```

Listing 8-13   `Collection` interface

The Collections Framework doesn't provide any direct implementations of the Collection interface. Instead, it provides implementations of more specific subinterfaces like Set and List. Some of these implementations allow duplicate elements and some don't. Similarly, some implementations are ordered and others are not. Features such as ordering and duplicate elimination have a performance cost, so you should select the collection type with the fewest features that still meets your needs.

8.4.4   List Objects

A List is an ordered collection, sometimes referred to as a sequence. List objects can contain duplicate elements. If you've used java.util.Vector, you're already familiar with the general characteristics of List. When using a List, you generally have precise control over where each element is inserted in the List. You can access elements in a list by their integer indexes.

Most of the time when you need a List, the ArrayList implementation is the best choice. ArrayList offers constant-time positional access and is quite fast. It doesn't have to allocate a node object for each element in the List and it uses the native method System.arraycopy to move multiple elements simultaneously. An ArrayList is essentially a Vector without the synchronization overhead.

ArrayList has one tuning parameter, its initial capacity. This is the number of elements that the ArrayList can hold before it has to grow. If you have a good idea how big the collection is, you can avoid unnecessary allocations when items are added to the collection by setting this parameter.

You might want to consider using LinkedList if you need to frequently add elements to the beginning of the List or iterate over the List and delete elements from its interior. These are constant-time operations in a LinkedList and linear-time operations in an ArrayList. However, keep in mind that this performance gain might be more than offset by other factors. Positional access can be much slower in a LinkedList—it's a linear-time operation in a LinkedList and a constant-time operation in an ArrayList. The fixed overhead for LinkedList operations is also much greater than for ArrayList operations.

The best way to decide which type of List to use is to create some benchmarks that reflect how the List is used in your program. Since ArrayList and LinkedList share the same interface, it's easy to swap implementations.

8.4.5   Set Objects

A Set is a collection that cannot contain duplicate elements. This interface models the mathematical abstraction *set*. It is used to represent sets like the cards in a poker hand, the courses that make up a student's schedule, or the processes running on a machine.

The two general-purpose `Set` implementations are `HashSet` and `TreeSet`. Deciding which to use is very straightforward. `HashSet` is much faster[4] but offers no ordering guarantees. If you need to use the operations in `SortedSet` or if in-order iteration is important to you, use `TreeSet`. Otherwise, use `HashSet`. You will probably use `HashSet` most of the time.

If iteration performance matters, it's important to choose an appropriate initial capacity for a `HashSet`. Choosing a capacity that's too high can waste space as well as time. (Iteration is linear in the sum of the number of entries and the capacity.) The default initial capacity is 101, which is often more than you need. In general, you should set the initial capacity to about twice the size that you expect the `Set` to grow to. If your estimate is way off, the `Set` might have to grow or you might waste a bit of space, but it won't have a big impact. If you know a prime number that's about the right size, use it. If not, use an odd number.

The initial capacity can be specified using the `int` constructor. For example, to construct a `HashSet` with an initial capacity of 17:

```
Set s= new HashSet(17);
```

`HashSet`s have one other tuning parameter, the *load factor*. This is a measure of how full the `HashSet` is allowed to get before its capacity is automatically increased. When the number of entries exceeds the product of the load factor and the current capacity, the capacity is doubled. Generally, the default load factor (.75) offers a good trade-off between time and space costs. Higher values decrease the space overhead, but increase the time it takes to look up an entry.

8.4.6   Map Objects

A `Map` is an object that maps keys to values. `Map`s cannot contain duplicate keys: each key can map to at most one value. If you've used `java.util.Hashtable`, you're already familiar with the general characteristics of `Map`. Using `Map` is analogous to using `Set`: If you need `SortedMap` operations or in-order collection-view iteration, use `TreeMap`; otherwise, use `HashMap`.

8.4.7   Synchronized Collections

The older data structure classes, `Hashtable` and `Vector`, are fully synchronized. Programs pay the costs associated with thread synchronization even when they're used in a single-threaded environment. By default, the classes in the Collections

---

4. O(1) instead of log(n) time for most operations.

Framework are *not* synchronized. This provides the fastest possible access to these structures when they're used in a single-threaded environment. The Collections Framework supports synchronized collections through a set of wrapper classes.

These wrapper classes add functionality to the standard `Collection` implementations, but delegate all of their real work to the standard implementations. Design patterns fans will recognize this as an example of the *Decorator* pattern.[5] The wrapper implementations are anonymous: Rather than exposing additional public classes, the API provides a static *factory method*[6] for each implementation. These factory methods, shown in Listing 8-14, are defined in the `Collections` class (not to be confused with the `Collection` interface).

```
public static Collection synchronizedCollection(Collection c);
public static Set synchronizedSet(Set s);
public static List synchronizedList(List list);
public static Map synchronizedMap(Map m);
public static SortedSet synchronizedSortedSet(SortedSet s);
public static SortedMap synchronizedSortedMap(SortedMap m);
```

Listing 8-14   Factory methods for synchronized collections

Each factory method returns a synchronized (thread-safe) `Collection` that is backed by an instance of the specified collection type. For example, to create a thread-safe `ArrayList` object, you call `Collections.synchronizedList`:

```
List list = Collections.synchronizedList(new ArrayList());
```

A `Collection` created in this fashion is every bit as thread-safe as a "normally" synchronized collection like a `Vector`. To guarantee serial access, however, it is critical that all access to the backing collection be done through the `Collection` returned by the factory method. The easiest solution is to avoid keeping a reference to the backing `Collection`.

When you iterate over a synchronized collection, you have to manually synchronize the iteration operation. This is because iteration is performed through multiple calls into the collection and these calls have to be composed into a single atomic operation. Listing 8-15 shows the proper technique for iterating over a wrapper-synchronized collection. *Failing to use this idiom can result in non-deterministic behavior.*

---

5. For more information about the Decorator pattern, see Erich Gamma, et al., *Design Patterns: Elements of Reusable Object-Oriented Software*, pp. 127–134. Addison-Wesley, 1995.
6. For more information about Factory methods, see Erich Gamma, et al., pp. 107–116.

```
Collection c = Collections.synchronizedCollection(myCollection);
synchronized(c) {
    Iterator i = c.iterator(); // Must be in synchronized block!
    while (i.hasNext())
        foo(i.next());
}
```

Listing 8-15   Iterating over a thread-safe collection

With these synchronization wrappers, you can get complete thread-safety when you need it without having to incur the overhead if you're working in a single-threaded environment.

8.4.8   Collections Framework Algorithms

The Collections Framework provides some common algorithms that operate on Collections. Two are particularly interesting from a performance perspective: sort and binarySearch. Sorting and searching are common tasks that can take up a great deal of time. The Collections Framework provides well-tested implementations of these tasks that have well-documented performance characteristics. For example, the sort method uses a merge sort[7] that provides good performance across a wide variety of situations.

These algorithm implementations are accessed through static utility methods defined in the Collections class. The method signatures are shown in Listing 8-16.

```
public static int binarySearch(List list, Object key);
public static int binarySearch(List list, Object key,
                               Comparator c);
public static void sort(List list) ;
public static void sort(List list, Comparator c);
```

Listing 8-16   Sorting and searching utilities

8.4.9   Plain Arrays

Most of the Collections Framework is geared toward handling collections of objects—all the methods in Collection are typed for Object. Many times, however, you need to work with primitive types such as int, double, and boolean. One approach is to use the object wrappers for primitive types such as Integer, Double, and Boolean and then insert them into the Collection. This works, but

---

7. For more information about merge sort, see Robert Sedgewick, *Algorithms (Second Edition)*, pp. 163–175. Addison-Wesley, 1988.

in performance-critical situations it's not a good solution. The overhead of allocating a wrapper for each primitive and then extracting the primitive value from the wrapper each time it's used is quite high. In performance-critical situations, a better solution is to work with plain array structures when you're dealing with collections of primitive types.

While working with plain arrays can be less convenient and more error-prone than using the `Collection` interface, the Collections Framework does include some utilities to make it easier. The `java.util.Arrays` class provides similar functionality to the `java.util.Collections` class. This class gives you access to the same well-tested, high-performance sorting and searching functions that you can use with other collections.

8.4.10   Immutable Collections

Chapter 7 addresses the importance of making informed decisions about object mutability. The ability to return immutable objects can be important when you're working with collections, which can be expensive to copy. The Collections Framework provides wrapper implementations you can use to make a collection immutable. These wrappers are similar to the synchronization wrappers. They simply intercept any operations that would modify the collection and throw an `UnsupportedOperationException`.

By making the collection returned by a method immutable, you can avoid the overhead of copying the collection while maintaining full encapsulation of your data.

Like the synchronization wrappers, there is one `static` factory method for each of the six core `Collection` interfaces, as shown in Listing 8-17. These methods reside in the `Collections` class.

```
public static Collection unmodifiableCollection(Collection c);
public static Set unmodifiableSet(Set s);
public static List unmodifiableList(List list);
public static Map unmodifiableMap(Map m);
public static SortedSet unmodifiableSortedSet(SortedSet s);
public static SortedMap unmodifiableSortedMap(SortedMap m);
```

Listing 8-17   Immutable collection wrappers

8.5   Collections Example

Throughout this chapter, we've emphasized how the algorithms and data structures you use can have a large impact on the performance of your software. To help illustrate this point, this section examines a simple benchmark that compares the speed of various implementations of the `Collection` interface. It demonstrates just how large an impact the choices you make can have on performance.

Listing 8-18 contains the benchmark we'll use to test the speed of different operations on a `Collection`.

```
public static void test(Collection c) {
   System.out.println("Testing "+c.getClass());
   Stopwatch timer = new Stopwatch().start();
   add(c);
   timer.stop();
   System.out.println("add: "+
                        timer.getElapsedTime());
   timer.reset().start();
   iterate(c);
   timer.stop();
   System.out.println("iter: "+
                        timer.getElapsedTime());
   if (c instanceof List) {
      List l = (List)c;
      timer.reset().start();
      randomAccess(l);
      timer.stop();
      System.out.println("random: "+
                        timer.getElapsedTime());
   }
   timer.reset().start();
   remove(c);
   timer.stop();
   System.out.println("remove: "+
                        timer.getElapsedTime());
}
```

Listing 8-18   Collections benchmark

The collection operations performed by this benchmark are shown in Listing 8-19. These methods test the speed of adding items to the collection, iterating over the collection, and removing items from the collection. For collections that also implement the `List` interface, a method is provided to test the speed of randomly accessing items. (This function is only tested on `List` objects because other collections don't provide a `get(int)` method.)

```
public static void add(Collection c) {
   for (int i = 0; i < NUM_ITEMS; i++) {
      c.add(objects[i]);
   }
}
public static void iterate(Collection c) {
   for (int i = 0; i < 100; i++) {
```

```
      Iterator iter = c.iterator();
      while (iter.hasNext()) {
         Object o = iter.next();
      }
   }
}
public static void remove(Collection c) {
   Iterator iter = c.iterator();
   while (iter.hasNext()) {
      Object o = iter.next();
      iter.remove();
   }
}
public static void randomAccess(List c) {
   for (int i = 0; i < NUM_ITEMS; i++) {
      Object o = c.get(random());
   }
}
```

Listing 8-19   Collection operations

8.5.1   Collection Benchmark Results

The collection benchmark defined in Section 8.5 can be used to perform basic performance testing on different implementations of the Collection interface. In this section, we examine the results for five classes:

- ArrayList
- LinkedList
- Vector
- TreeSet
- HashSet

Listing 8-20 shows how instances of these classes are created and passed to the benchmark for testing.

```
public static void main(String[] args) {
   Collection arrayList = new ArrayList();
   test(arrayList);
   Collection linkedList = new LinkedList();
   test(linkedList);
   Collection vector = new Vector();
   test(vector);
   Collection treeSet = new TreeSet();
   test(treeSet);
   Collection hashSet = new HashSet();
   test(hashSet);
}
```

Listing 8-20   Testing the collections

Random Numbers in Benchmarks

The randomAccess method in Listing 8-19 contains a call to a method called random. The initial version of this benchmark used the java.util.Random class to generate the random index for the item to retrieve. However, it turned out that generating the random numbers sometimes took longer than getting the items. Since we wanted to focus on the performance characteristics of the List, not the random number generator, this version of the benchmark uses a different approach. A large array of random numbers is created at start-up time and the random method simply pulls them out of the array during the timed part of the test. This helped focus the results of the benchmark on the List behavior.

Table 8-1 shows how long it took to execute each test on our test configuration. Note that columns that contain 0 indicate that the time it took to execute the test was below the resolution of the System.getCurrentMillis timer. (In other words, these operations were really fast.)

Class	Add	Iterate	Random	Remove
ArrayList	0 ms	660 ms	0 ms	2,360 ms
LinkedList	50 ms	1,100 ms	26,800 ms	0 ms
Vector	0 ms	880 ms	0 ms	2,580 ms
TreeSet	330 ms	1,430 ms	N/A	60 ms
HashSet	110 ms	1,430 ms	N/A	50 ms

Table 8-1   Collection Benchmark Results

These results illustrate how important the selection of algorithms and data structures can be. Look at the results from the different List implementations. ArrayList and Vector, two similar classes that are both array-based structures, show similar performance characteristics. Since Vector provides synchronization by default, it's slightly slower. If you compare the ArrayList and LinkedList results, however, you'll see that they have very different performance characteristics. While these two structures are capable of performing the same operations, operations that are practically free on the ArrayList are very costly with the

LinkedList and vice-versa. The results also show how the set-based structures have very different performance characteristics from the list-based structures.

As you can see from this simple benchmark, you need to understand how your data structures will be used before settling on any particular implementation. Abstractions such as the Collection interface make it fairly easy to try several alternatives, and benchmarking and profiling will help you identify which is best.

8.6   References on Algorithms and Data Structures

Abrash, Michael. *Graphics Programming Black Book, Special Edition*, The Coriolis Group, Scottsdale, AZ, 1997.

Binstock, Andrew and John Rex. *Practical Algorithms for Programmers*, Addison-Wesley, Reading, MA, 1995.

Sedgewick, Robert. *Algorithms (Second Edition)*, Addison-Wesley, Reading, MA, 1988.

Key Points

- The performance of any algorithm or data structure depends on the context in which it is used.

- You must consider your problem domain when designing or selecting algorithms.

- Recursion can be a useful tool and might be less costly than you expect.

- The Collections Framework provides pretested, high-performance algorithms and data structures that can be used in many common situations.

- The Collections Framework gives you a high degree of control over synchronization and mutability.

CHAPTER 9

Using Native Code

MUCH of the older literature on performance tuning for the Java platform encourages developers to write C code when truly peak performance is required. While this was reasonable advice in a world without JIT compilers, it is less likely a good solution today. You might need to write native code if your application requires access to platform features not supported in the Java libraries. However, when motivated purely by performance, it is not usually a good idea to glue C code into your Java program. It turns out that the overhead of crossing the Java/C boundary is so severe that it more than compensates for the small performance gains you might realize by moving code to C.

The examples shown in this chapter use the Java Native Interface (JNI) mechanism to glue the Java language code and the C language code together. For more information about JNI, see *The Java Native Interface: Programmer's Guide and Specification.*[1]

This chapter starts with a substantial example of porting an algorithm written with the Java language to C. Although this is a complex numerical algorithm, of the type people are often encouraged to code in C, the performance of the C version turns out to be poor. Section 9.2 takes a more detailed look at the various costs associated with using JNI, and describes several different patterns used to write native code—some that can be fast and some that are generally slow. Section 9.3 finishes up the chapter by looking at a few case studies that highlight decisions about using native code.

9.1 Native Graphics Example

In Chapter 8, a complex algorithm for drawing arbitrary lines, Bresenham's algorithm, is used to illustrate the importance of algorithm selection. In this section, we code Bresenham's algorithm in C so we can compare the performance of Java language and the C language implementations of the same algorithm. Listing 9-1

---

1. Sheng Liang, *The Java Native Interface: Programmer's Guide and Specification.* Addison-Wesley, 1999.

129

shows the "glue" object used to interface with the native C code. Listing 9-2 shows the C implementation of Bresenham's algorithm.

```java
public class DowncodedBresenham implements LineDrawer {
    static {
        try {
            System.loadLibrary("bresenham");
        } catch (Exception e) {
            e.printStackTrace();
        }
    }
    public native void drawLine(BufferedImage i,
                                int x0, int y0,
                                int x1, int y1);
}
```

Listing 9-1   Interface to the native drawing code

```c
#include "DowncodedBresenham.h"

static jclass biclass = NULL;
static jmethodID bimid;

// macro to call pixel set on bufferedimage
#define SETRGB(bi,x,y,rgbval) \
    env->CallVoidMethod(bi,bimid,x,y,rgbval)

static void octant0(JNIEnv *env,jobject bi, jint x0, jint y0,
                    int dx, int dy, int xdirection);
static void octant1(JNIEnv *env,jobject bi, jint x0, jint y0,
                    int dx, int dy, int xdirection);

JNIEXPORT void JNICALL Java_DowncodedBresenham_drawLine
    (JNIEnv *env, jobject thisObj, jobject bufferedImage,
     jint x0, jint y0, jint x1, jint y1){
    int temp,dx,dy;
    // set up class and method pointers
    if (biclass == NULL) {
        biclass = env->GetObjectClass(bufferedImage);
        bimid = env->GetMethodID(biclass,"setRGB","(III)V");
    }
    // reduce to half the octant cases by always drawing + in y
    if (y0>y1) {
        temp = y0;
        y0 = y1;
        y1 = temp;
        temp = x0;
        x0 = x1;
        x1 = temp;
    }
    dx = x1-x0;
```

```
      dy = y1-y0;
      if (dx>0) {
         if (dx>dy) {
            octant0(env,bufferedImage,x0,y0,dx,dy,1);
         } else {
            octant1(env,bufferedImage,x0,y0,dx,dy,1);
         }
      } else {
         dx = -dx;
         if (dx>dy) {
            octant0(env,bufferedImage,x0,y0,dx,dy,-1);
         } else {
            octant1(env,bufferedImage,x0,y0,dx,dy,-1);
         }
      }
}

static void octant0(JNIEnv *env,jobject bi, jint x0, jint y0,
                    int dx, int dy, int xdirection){
      int DeltaYx2;
      int DeltaYx2MinusDeltaXx2;
      int ErrorTerm;
      jint pix = 0xffffffff;
      // set up initial error term and drawing values
      DeltaYx2 = dy*2;
      DeltaYx2MinusDeltaXx2 = DeltaYx2 - (dx*2);
      ErrorTerm = DeltaYx2 - dx;
      // draw loop
      //bi.setRGB(x0,y0,pix); // draws a single point
      SETRGB(bi,x0,y0,pix);
      while ( dx-- > 0) {
         // check if we need to advance y
         if (ErrorTerm >=0) {
         // advance Y and reset ErrorTerm
            y0++;
            ErrorTerm += DeltaYx2MinusDeltaXx2;
         } else {
         // add error to ErrorTerm
            ErrorTerm += DeltaYx2;
         }
         x0 += xdirection;
         //bi.setRGB(x0,y0,pix);
         SETRGB(bi,x0,y0,pix);
      }
}

static void octant1(JNIEnv *env,jobject bi, jint x0, jint y0,
                    int dx, int dy,
                    int xdirection){
      int DeltaXx2;
      int DeltaXx2MinusDeltaYx2;
      int ErrorTerm;
      jint pix = 0xffffffff;
      // set up initial error term and drawing values
```

```
DeltaXx2 = dx * 2;
DeltaXx2MinusDeltaYx2 = DeltaXx2 - (dy*2);
ErrorTerm = DeltaXx2- dy;
// draw loop
//bi.setRGB(x0,y0,pix);
SETRGB(bi,x0,y0,pix);
while ( dy-- > 0) {
    // check if we need to advance x
    if (ErrorTerm >= 0) {
        // advance X and reset ErrorTerm
        x0 += xdirection;
        ErrorTerm += DeltaXx2MinusDeltaYx2;
    } else {
        // add to ErrorTerm
        ErrorTerm += DeltaXx2;
    }
    y0++;
    //bi.setRGB(x0,y0,pix);
    SETRGB(bi,x0,y0,pix);
}
}
```

Listing 9-2   C implementation of `LineDrawer`

The relative performance of the Java language and C language versions of Bresenham's algorithm can be measured using the wrapper shown in Listing 9-3.

```
import java.lang.reflect.*;

public class GridApp{

    public static void main(String args[]) {
        if (Array.getLength(args)<1) {
            System.out.println("usage: TrivialApplication b|d");
            System.exit(0);
        }
        if ((args[0].startsWith("b"))||(args[0].startsWith("B")))
            new GridTest(new BasicBreshenham());
        else
            new GridTest(new DowncodedBresenham());
    }
}
```

Listing 9-3   Micro-benchmark for line drawing

9.1.1   Native Code Comparison

On our test configuration, the native version of Bresenham's algorithm is about 75 percent slower than the Java language version. This seems to contradict the conventional wisdom that says you should rewrite complex algorithmic code in C for optimum performance. Why doesn't the C version run faster?

The comparison of the line drawing implementations illustrates two things:

- For implementing complex, purely numerical computations, the Java programming language isn't a bad choice. For these types of problems, a competent JIT gives you speed that is at least competitive with C code. In addition, next generation runtime systems, such as the HotSpot VM, can use dynamic runtime information to produce highly optimized code, taking advantage of optimizations not available to C and C++ compilers. This is especially true when you're working with object-oriented code.

- There is a lot of overhead associated with invoking native code through JNI. When you call JNI code you are in effect asking the JVM to reach out to pieces of code outside of its normal operating environment. When the C code calls back into the Java environment, a similar transition must occur. These transition costs are described in the next section.

9.2   Examining JNI Costs

When JNI is used to hook native code into an application, there are a few patterns that are commonly used. This section discusses four common patterns—most JNI code follows one of these patterns, or uses some combination of these patterns. Each pattern can have a very different performance profile.

Note: The performance costs of the different JNI patterns tend to be very platform and JVM dependent. The benchmark results in this chapter are illustrative of the results you might see on a JVM implementation that supports JNI, but specific results and relative costs might differ widely under different configurations.

Listing 9-4 shows several examples of the different JNI patterns. These examples help illustrate some of the costs associated with accessing native code.

```
public class TrivialApplication {
   static {
      try {
         System.loadLibrary("copytest");
      } catch (Exception e) {
         e.printStackTrace();
      }
   }
}
```

```java
public static void main(String args[]) {
    long time;
    int[] intarray = new int[1000];
    int[] intarray2 = new int[1000];
    Stopwatch watch = new Stopwatch().start();
    for (int i=0;i<100000;i++) {
        System.arraycopy(intarray,0,intarray2,0,1000);
    }
    time =watch.getElapsedTime();
    System.out.println("arraycopy() = "+time);
    watch.reset().start();
    for (int i=0;i<100000;i++) {
        for (int j=0;j<1000;j++) {
            intarray2[j] = intarray[j];
        }
    }
    time = watch.getElapsedTime();
    System.out.println("assign = "+time);
    watch.reset().start();
    for (int i=0;i<100000;i++) {
        dumbnativecopy(intarray,intarray2,1000);
    }
    time =watch.getElapsedTime();
    System.out.println("dumbnativecopy() ="+time);
    watch.reset().start();
    for (int i=0;i<100000;i++) {
        nativedonothing(intarray,intarray2,1000);
    }
    time =watch.getElapsedTime();
    System.out.println("nativedonothing() ="+time);
    watch.reset().start();
    for (int i=0;i<100000;i++) {
        nativedoabsolutelynothing(intarray,intarray2,1000);
    }
    time =watch.getElapsedTime();
    System.out.println("nativedoabsolutelynothing()= "+time);
    watch.reset().start();
    for (int i=0;i<100000;i++) {
        nativecritical(intarray,intarray2,1000);
    }
    time =watch.getElapsedTime();
    System.out.println("nativecritical() ="+time);
    watch.reset().start();
    for (int i=0;i<100000;i++) {
        nativecriticalmemcpy(intarray,intarray2,1000);
    }
    time =watch.getElapsedTime();
    System.out.println("timeusing nativecriticalmemcpy() ="+time);
    watch.stop();
}
public static native void dumbnativecopy(int[] i1,
                                         int[] i2,
                                         int size);
public static native void lessdumbnativecopy(int[] i1,
```

```
                                                int[] i2,
                                                int size);
        public static native void nativedonothing(int[] i1,
                                                int[] i2,
                                                int size);
        public static native void nativedoabsolutelynothing(int[] i1,
                                                int[] i2,
                                                int size);
        public static native void nativecritical(int[] i1,
                                                int[] i2,
                                                int size);
        public static native void nativecriticalmemcpy(int[] i1,
                                                int[] i2,
                                                int size);

}
```

Listing 9-4   Array copy JNI test

In Listing 9-4, a number of different techniques are used to copy an array that contains 1,000 elements. The copy operations are performed using various native and nonnative methods. To make it easier to compare the performance of these different techniques, the program performs each copy 10,000 times.

The first two copy techniques don't use any native code; the rest call C functions. These C functions are written using different JNI usage patterns to illustrate the costs associated with different coding techniques. Note that some of these C functions don't perform the full array copy; they're included to highlight the costs of particular operations. Table 9-1 shows the benchmark results for the different methods.

Copy Method	Time
arraycopy	234 ms
assign	984 ms
dumbnativecopy	1,609 ms
nativedonothing	1,125 ms
nativedoabsolutelynothing	63 ms
nativecritical	578 ms
nativecriticalmemcpy	422 ms
nativepullonly	391 ms

Table 9-1   Array Copy Results

9.2.1   Java Language Copy

The first two options require no C code at all. The `assign` method uses a simple Java language loop to perform the copy. This isn't the fastest option, but it isn't the slowest either. The other nonnative option is to use the `System.arraycopy` method. This turns out to be the fastest way to perform the copy. The next few sections examine why this is the case.

9.2.2   JNI Patterns

Each of the C functions in the array copy example follows a common JNI usage pattern. The next few sections look at the impact of using these patterns in the array copy example and discuss the performance implications of each pattern.

9.2.3   Pattern 1: Call

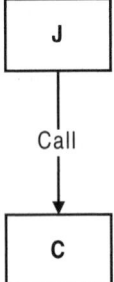

Figure 9-1   Call pattern

The simplest JNI pattern is the Call pattern. In this pattern, you simply call a C function, pass along primitive arguments, and expect a primitive return type. A diagram of this pattern is shown in Figure 9-1.

   This pattern can be quite efficient in certain circumstances. Listing 9-5 shows an example of this pattern, the `nativedoabsolutelynothing` method.

```
JNIEXPORT void JNICALL
java_TrivialApplication_nativedoabsolutelynothing
   (JNIEnv *env, jclass myclass,
    jintArray i1, jintArray i2, jint size) {
    // Do nothing
}
```

Listing 9-5   Call example

While the `nativedoabsolutelynothing` method doesn't actually do anything, there still is a cost associated with it. In our measurements, it took 63 milliseconds to call this method 10,000 times. This might not seem like much, but compared to the `System.arraycopy` method it's a significant amount of time.

It is most appropriate to use this pattern when you have a considerable amount of work to do inside the C code. The more work you do in the C code, the less important the overhead of the JVM to C call is. However, many problems require the use of nonprimitive data (such as arrays or objects). In these cases, you can't use this pattern.

9.2.4 Pattern 2: Call-Pull

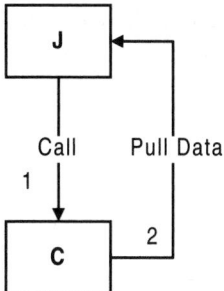

Figure 9-2   Call-Pull pattern

When you use the Call-Pull pattern, you call a native function that pulls a complex data type, such as an array or an object, from the JVM. This pattern is illustrated in Figure 9-2. Note that the arrows show the directions of the calls, not the direction that the data moves.

In the Call-Pull example in Listing 9-6, the method is passed pointers to the Java language array structures. Before it can actually manipulate the contents of the arrays, however, it has to make a local copy of the data by calling the `GetIntArrayRegion` method. This method reaches back up into the JVM to copy the requested data, which is quite expensive.

In our tests, it took almost 400 milliseconds to call this method 10,000 times. That is much longer than the entire copy took using `arraycopy`, and this method doesn't actually return a new copy of the array. As you'll see in the next section, that takes even longer.

This extra expense is required to ensure thread safety. If you have your own copy of the data, then you don't need to worry about some other thread (such as the garbage collector) altering your data while you're working on it.

```
JNIEXPORT void JNICALL Java_TrivialApplication_nativepullonly
            (JNIEnv *env, jclass myclass,
             jintArray i1, jintArray i2, jint size){
    long *int1;
    int1 = (long *)malloc(sizeof(long)*size);
    env->GetIntArrayRegion(i1,0,size,int1);
    free(int1);
}
```

Listing 9-6   Call-Pull example

The Call-Pull pattern can be appropriate if you have a piece of complex data and just need to return a simple result—for example, if you needed to take a block of data, perform complex statistical analysis on that data, and then return a primitive result. However, the cost of bringing down the data can outweigh any benefit you get from translating to C code. If you choose to write native code using this pattern, you need to carefully measure its performance to make sure you're getting a net benefit.

9.2.5   Pattern 3: Call-Pull-Push

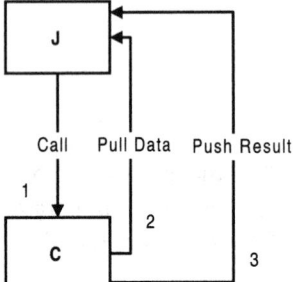

Figure 9-3   Call-Pull-Push pattern

Call-Pull-Push is a common pattern in JNI code. In fact, this is the pattern that is required to actually fully accomplish an array copy operation. This pattern is illustrated in Figure 9-3.

The `nativedonothing` method in Listing 9-7 is the simplest example of this pattern. Like the example in Listing 9-5, the `GetIntArrayRegion` is used to create a local copy of the array. This version then adds a call to `SetIntArrayRegion` to push the data back to the JVM.

```
JNIEXPORT void JNICALL Java_TrivialApplication_nativedonothing
    (JNIEnv *env, jclass myclass,
     jintArray i1, jintArray i2, jint size) {
    long *int1;
    long *int2;
    int1 = (long *)malloc(sizeof(long)*size);
    int2 = (long *)malloc(sizeof(long)*size);
    env->GetIntArrayRegion(i1,0,size,int1);
    env->SetIntArrayRegion(i2,0,size,int2);
    free(int1);
    free(int2);
}
```

Listing 9-7 `nativedonothing`

Despite the fact that the `nativedonothing` function does no useful work, it is still very time-consuming. The amount of time consumed by this method was even greater than the very naive Java programming language loop copy, and was several times more expensive than `System.arraycopy` version.

Listing 9-8 includes the first native function that fully performs the array copy. It uses the same get and put calls as the previous example, but also adds a loop to copy the array. It is interesting to note that the version that actually copies the array is only 40 percent slower than the version that does nothing. That gives you an idea of how large the overhead of copying these arguments can be.

```
JNIEXPORT void JNICALL Java_TrivialApplication_dumbnativecopy
    (JNIEnv *env, jclass myclass,
     jintArray i1, jintArray i2, jint size){
    long *int1;
    long *int2;
    int1 = (long *)malloc(sizeof(long)*size);
    int2 = (long *)malloc(sizeof(long)*size);
    env->GetIntArrayRegion(i1,0,size,int1);
    for (int i=0;i<size;i++) {
       int2[i] = int1[i];
    }
    env->SetIntArrayRegion(i2,0,size,int2);
    free(int1);
    free(int2);
}
```

Listing 9-8 `dumbnativecopy`

9.2.6   Pattern 3 (Variant): Call-Pull-Push with Critical

The previous sections show that using native code that accesses complex data types is very expensive. This is because these arguments must be copied to local storage inside the C heap to provide thread safety. In limited circumstances, however, it is possible to avoid this overhead, which can drastically improve performance.

JNI includes what are called *critical accessor* functions. These functions give your native code direct access to data structures inside the Java object heap, without requiring that they be copied. This results in a substantial performance boost. An example of this pattern is shown in Listing 9-9. To access the data, the GetPrimitiveArrayCritical method is used.

```
JNIEXPORT void JNICALL Java_TrivialApplication_nativecritical
(JNIEnv *env, jclass myclass,
 jintArray i1, jintArray i2, jint size){
   int *int1 = (int *)env->GetPrimitiveArrayCritical(i1,0);
   int *int2 = (int *)env->GetPrimitiveArrayCritical(i2,0);
   int count = size*sizeof(jint)/sizeof(int);
   int *iptr1 = int1;
   int *iptr2 = int2;
   for (int i=0;i<count;i++) {
      *iptr2++ = *iptr1++;
   }
   env->ReleasePrimitiveArrayCritical(i1,int1,0);
   env->ReleasePrimitiveArrayCritical(i2,int2,0);
}
```

Listing 9-9 nativecritical

In this case, using the critical methods speeds up the array copy by nearly three times. This speedup is due to the fact that the data isn't copied to local storage. But how do these critical methods maintain thread safety if the data isn't copied? The answer to this question reveals the limitations of this solution. When you use a critical method to access data inside a native method, all threads inside the JVM are blocked to maintain thread safety.

This includes not only user threads, but threads such as the garbage collector. This means that you cannot use these critical methods in a native function that might block. For example, if the method touches the file system, video memory, or any other structures that might have locks held by threads inside the JVM, then your program can deadlock. If more than a few milliseconds is spent in such a method, it's also possible to block threads, such as the user interface thread, in a manner that can make the user think the program has crashed. If you can work within these constraints, however, these methods can be a big boon to performance.

For completeness, there is one more native function to discuss—nativecriticalmemcpy, which is shown in Listing 9-10. This is the fastest way to write the array copy functionality using JNI. It uses the critical functions to access the data, as shown in the previous example. However, it replaces the loop with a call to the standard C memcpy function. This low-level call is optimized for just this kind of work, and in fact provides a 25 percent speedup over the previous example.

```
JNIEXPORT void JNICALL
Java_TrivialApplication_nativecriticalmemcpy
    (JNIEnv *env, jclass myclass,
     jintArray i1, jintArray i2, jint size){
    int *int1 = (int *)env->GetPrimitiveArrayCritical(i1,0);
    int *int2 = (int *)env->GetPrimitiveArrayCritical(i2,0);
    int count = size*sizeof(jint)/sizeof(int);
    int *iptr1 = int1;
    int *iptr2 = int2;
    memcpy(iptr2,iptr1,count*sizeof(int));
    env->ReleasePrimitiveArrayCritical(i1,int1,0);
    env->ReleasePrimitiveArrayCritical(i2,int2,0);
}
```

Listing 9-10 `nativecriticalmemcopy`

Despite the fact that the critical methods can provide a substantial performance boost, the fastest native version of this method is still slower than the version that uses `System.arraycopy`. This is because `System.arrayCopy` is designed to work with full knowledge of the JVM's internals, and doesn't incur any of the overhead suffered by normal JNI calls.

9.2.7   Pattern 4: Call-Invoke

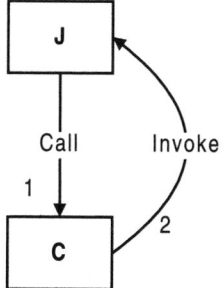

Figure 9-4   Call-Invoke pattern

One more pattern that is commonly found in JNI code is Call-Invoke. In this pattern, the JVM calls a native method, which in turn calls one or more Java language methods. This pattern is illustrated in Figure 9-4.

The native Bresenham line drawing example shown at the beginning of this chapter uses this pattern. The line drawing native method is called, and then repeatedly calls a Java method to manipulate the pixels in the buffered image.

As you recall, the Bresenham example was substantially slower when coded in C than with the Java programming language. The Call-Invoke pattern often leads to performance problems. When you create native methods that call Java methods, you are likely to have performance problems. You generally are better off writing the code entirely in the Java programming language.

Why does the Call-Invoke pattern typically show poor results? The main reason is that invoking a Java language method from C uses a mechanism similar to the JVM reflection mechanism. Reflective method lookup and dispatch is fine for many uses, but if you're coding in C to improve performance, then the last thing you want to be doing is using reflection to invoke methods.

9.3   Native Code Case Studies

The examples in this chapter show that the decisions involved in moving performance critical code to C are complex. Profiling and benchmarking are key tools for deciding whether or not to use native code. However, the experiences that other developers have had can also be helpful. This section contains three brief case studies of projects that faced decisions regarding whether or not to use native code.

9.3.1   Java Media Framework

The Java Media Framework (JMF) 2.0 release supports video codecs[2] that perform complex, nonsequential, repeated operations on large arrays of data. The JMF team experimented with a variety of solutions, in some cases writing the same codec in both the Java and C languages. They found cases where moving to native code did improve performance. When these codecs were implemented in C, they ran between 15 and 20 percent faster, which was a significant gain for certain types of applications.

A cross-platform implementation of JMF that runs on any standard runtime environment is currently available. However, there are also performance packs available for the Windows and Solaris platforms that use native code for selected codecs. When downloading the JMF bundle, you can choose between the

---

2. *Codec* is an abbreviation of coder/decoder, the part of the system that compresses and decompresses media data.

cross-platform implementation and the version with the performance pack for your platform.

9.3.2   The `java.math` Package

During the development of J2SE v. 1.3 the decision was made to rewrite the `java.math` package. This package contains classes for doing mathematical operations on very large numbers and contains many complex numerical algorithms. Previous versions of this code had been written almost entirely in C, but this made maintenance complex, so the code was rewritten using the Java programming language. However, it was critical that performance not suffer.

During the project it became clear that the JNI overhead for some operations was very high. Most lightweight operations became substantially faster when translated into Java code. In addition, removing the C code made the design so much cleaner that it was possible to change the implementation to use more efficient algorithms. For an example of one of these algorithmic changes see Section 7.5, Mutable Object Case Study.

When the project was completed, benchmarks showed that most operations were much faster in the Java programming language version than they were in the C version. In many cases, operations were several hundred percent faster.

9.3.3   Java 3D

The Java 3D™ API is designed to allow programmers to create high-performance 3D graphics. It uses native code in order to interface with low-level graphics APIs such as OpenGL. Interfacing directly with OpenGL allows Java 3D to take advantage of the ability of many video cards to accelerate certain types of operations. Operations performed directly by the video hardware are much faster than operations that are performed in software (whether written with the Java programming language or C). This access to hardware acceleration is crucial for Java 3D to provide maximum performance. Getting access to special hardware can be a compelling reason to work with native code.

If you're interested in writing high-performance software with Java 3D, see the *Java 3D Performance Guide* at *http://java.sun.com/products/java-media/3D/collateral/j3d_perguide.html.*

Key Points

- The performance benefits of translating your Java code into C can be less than you think. It can even hurt your overall performance.

- The Call-Pull and Call-Pull-Push patterns of JNI usage add substantial overhead, and code that uses these patterns might perform poorly.

- The critical functions for accessing data can speed up the Call-Pull and Call-Pull-Push patterns, but there are major limitations on when they can be used safely.

- The Call-Invoke pattern often exhibits poor performance.

- Measure carefully when considering using native code.

CHAPTER 10

Swing Models and Renderers

THE Java Foundation Classes (JFC) Swing toolkit (Swing) provides a comprehensive set of classes for creating highly interactive graphical user interfaces with the Java platform. Swing is highly flexible, but also quite complex. While novice programmers can successfully use Swing to create basic graphical user interfaces (GUIs), to create a truly complex, professional-quality GUI you must understand Swing's architectural underpinnings. This is especially true when using Swing's more complex, renderer-based components such as JTable, JTree, JComboBox, and JList. The control provided by Swing's models and renderers is critical to writing high-performance, scalable GUIs.

This chapter provides an overview of Swing's component architecture, and explains how renderer objects extend this architecture to support components that display large datasets. Section 10.2 presents some tactics for improving performance by writing your code with knowledge of Swing's models in mind. Section 10.2.3 walks through a sample spreadsheet application that uses custom models and renderers to improve performance and reduce footprint.

10.1   Swing's Component Architecture

The original UI toolkit for the Smalltalk system used a pattern known as Model-View-Controller (MVC). MVC introduced the concept that a data source should be isolated from its onscreen representation. This is a powerful architecture that enables improved code reuse and program architectures. Swing uses a modified version of the MVC architecture, shown in Figure 10-1.

Typical Swing GUI components consist of at least three objects: a Component, a Model, and a UI Delegate. In Swing's architecture, the Model is charged with storing the data, while the UI Delegate is responsible for getting data from the Model and rendering it to the screen. The Component generally coordinates the actions of the Model and Delegate, while also acting as glue to the AWT windowing system.

Note that the UI Delegate can be replaced at runtime. This enables Swing's pluggable look-and-feel (PLAF) system, illustrated in Figure 10-2.

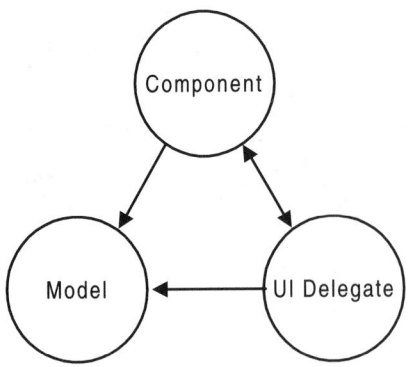

Figure 10-1   Swing component architecture

While Swing's modified MVC architecture clearly provides benefits in terms of flexibility, it has often been fingered as the cause of poor performance for some applications. Although it is true that an MVC-based architecture uses more method invocations to support the extra level of indirection, this cost is minimal.

Profiling Swing-based applications shows that the overhead for model-view separation is literally lost in the noise—it's less than one percent of CPU

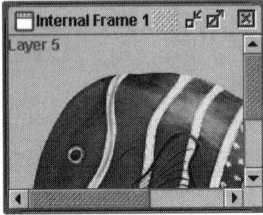

Java Look-and-Feel

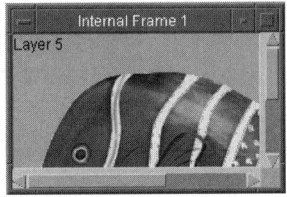

Motif Look-and-Feel

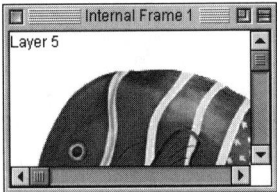

Mac OS Look-and-Feel

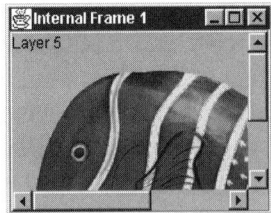

Windows Look-and-Feel

Figure 10-2   Swing's PLAF system

consumption. (The bulk of processing time for a complex Swing-based user interface is actually spent on low-level graphics operations.) Rather than being a cause of poor performance, Swing's model-view architecture is critical for building scalable programs.

10.2   Scalable Components

Swing provides a number of GUI components that are designed to manipulate datasets that are potentially very large, including

- JTable
- JTree
- JList
- JComboBox

These scalable components are designed to be able to manipulate thousands, or even millions of pieces of data. To do this without using massive amounts of memory, these components add the concept of a *renderer* to Swing's architecture. Figure 10-3 shows the modified architecture.

10.2.1   Renderers

In these more complex Swing components, the renderer is key for providing scalability. Let's look at JTable as an example of why renderers exist. A naively implemented table might use a JLabel for each cell in the table. While this might work for small datasets, it doesn't work for large ones. For example, if you tried to

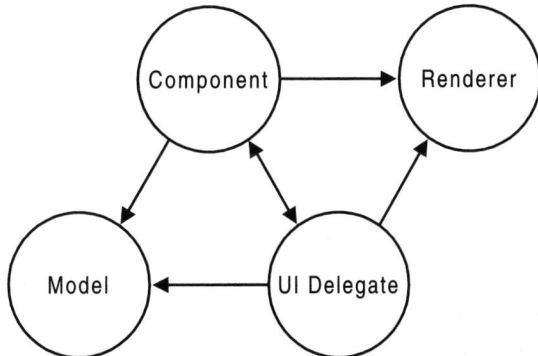

Figure 10-3   Scalable component architecture

display a 1,000 row by 1,000 column spreadsheet with such a table, the RAM requirements might be close to a *gigabyte,* even if every cell is empty.

To get around this scalability problem, Swing's JTable uses a single component to paint all of the cells that contain a particular data type. For example, all cells that contain String objects are drawn by the same component. This type of component is called a *renderer.* Using a renderer to display multiple cells drastically reduces the storage requirements for a large table.

When renderers are used to display a table, the data for a cell is fetched from the model, a renderer is configured based on that data, and then the cell is painted. The renderer is then moved to the location of the next cell and the process is repeated. The procedure is shown in Figure 10-4.

It's important to note that you can control this process by manipulating the renderers and models. All of the scalable components, such as JTree and JList, use this renderer approach; it isn't limited to JTable.

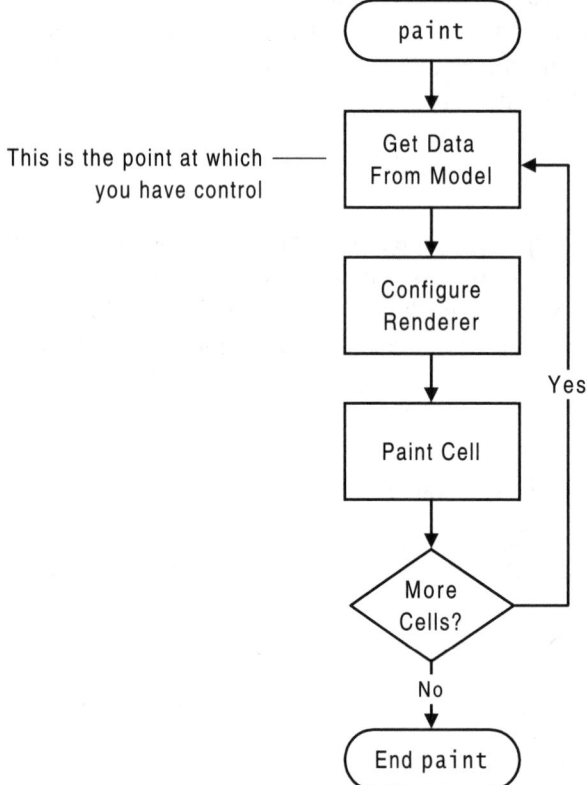

Figure 10-4   Rendering a component

10.2.2 Models

The ability to manipulate Swing models directly is critical for writing scalable user interfaces. As a simple example, take a look at Listing 10-1.

```
JComboBox box = new JComboBox();
for (int i = 0; i < numItems; i++) {
    box.addItem(new Integer(i));
}
```

Listing 10-1   Adding items to a `JComboBox`

This code simply adds a number of items to a `JComboBox`. The code is similar to the code you would use to load items into an AWT `Choice` box. This approach works fine for small numbers of items, but its inefficiency becomes apparent when a large number of items are added.

Although Listing 10-1 does not explicitly reference any models, the `JComboBox` object's model is involved. Each time you call `addItem` on the `JComboBox`, a fairly substantial amount of work is done—the component passes the request to the `JComboBox` model and the model posts an event to indicate that an item has been added. It turns out that you can accomplish the same thing much more efficiently by directly accessing the model, as shown in Listing 10-2.

```
Vector v = new Vector(numItems);
for (int i = 0; i < numItems; i++) {
    v.add(new Integer(i));
}
ComboBoxModel model = new DefaultComboBoxModel(v);
JComboBox box = new JComboBox(model);
```

Listing 10-2   Faster `JComboBox` loading

Why is this faster? The reason is twofold. First, because all the items are added to the model at once instead of one by one, only one event needs to be posted. This means that fewer event objects are created and fewer methods are called. Second, because fewer objects need to be notified of changes, less work is required. In general, the amount of work done equals the number of notifications multiplied by the number of listeners. Since the model is newly created, the number of listeners is zero, which means that no notifications are posted.

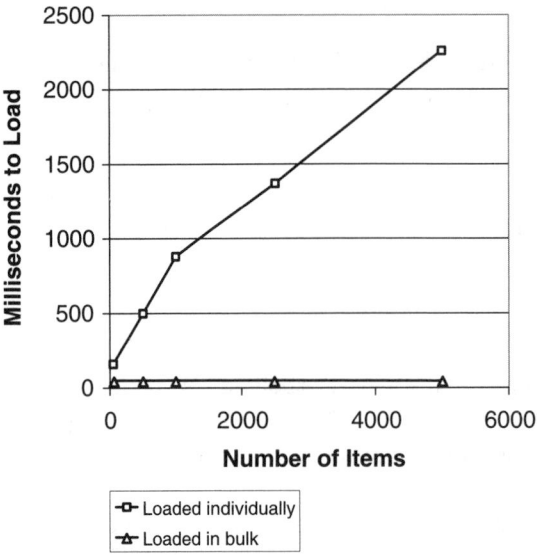

Figure 10-5   Combo box load times

There are two lessons to be learned here:

• Where possible, perform operations in bulk to reduce the number of events that are posted.

• When initializing or totally replacing the contents of a model, consider constructing a new one instead of reusing the existing one.

Configuration Differences

Throughout this book, we emphasize the fact that benchmark results are different depending on the configuration. The JComboBox loading benchmark is a classic example of this. Although the performance of loading items one-by-one is shown to be poor by this benchmark, it can be even worse. The version of Swing in J2SE v. 1.3 includes many optimizations, including improvements to JComboBox. Where it only took about 500 milliseconds to run the benchmark under version 1.3, it took more than 69 seconds to load 500 items when this benchmark was run under the Java 2 SDK v. 1.2.2.

So, how much faster is it to avoid the extra notifications? Figure 10-5 shows the results of using the examples in Listing 10-1 and Listing 10-2 to load different numbers of items.

As you can see, the first option scales very poorly. In fact, it takes more than two seconds to load 5,000 items into the JComboBox using the first approach. Loading the model in bulk takes a mere 50 milliseconds.

The number of notifications can have a large effect on your program's start-up time. It can also affect the amount of time it takes to open dialog boxes and perform similar operations.

10.2.3   Example: Simple Spreadsheet

A simple spreadsheet example, SheetMetal, is used in the following sections to illustrate several optimizations that can be made through creative use of renderers and models. The SheetMetal UI is shown in Figure 10-6.

Many of the optimizations described are application-specific. Some result in small improvements in performance, and others result in significant improvements. These optimizations illustrate the types of performance improvements you can make. They aren't meant to imply that you should make these specific optimizations in your own code; instead, they're designed to help you understand Swing's component architecture and make your own custom optimizations.

	A	B	C	D	E
1			3		
2	201			204	
3		402			405
4			603		
5	801			804	
6		1002			1005
7			1203		
8	1401			1404	
9		1602			1605
10			1803		
11	2001			2004	
12		2202			2205
13			2403		
14	2601			2604	
15		2802			2805
16			3003		
17	3201			3204	
18		3402			3405
19			3603		
20	3801			3804	

Figure 10-6   SheetMetal spreadsheet application

10.2.4   Using Custom Models

Swing contains a number of default models, such as DefaultTableModel. These models are generic and are suited to a wide variety of light-duty uses. For example, the DefaultTableModel is implemented internally as a Vector of Vector objects. It is quite usable for small data sets. However, it is clearly not the fastest or most space-efficient data structure. In general, when dealing with complex datasets, you should create your own custom model. The Swing model-view architecture was designed to give you this flexibility.

Let's look at the model requirements for the SheetMetal application. Spreadsheets are often used to hold very large datasets. For this example, we'll assume SheetMetal must be able to handle a dataset that contains 1,000 rows and 1,000 columns. If this functionality were implemented with the DefaultTableModel, the RAM requirements would be huge. DefaultTableModel is implemented using Vector, and Vector is implemented in terms of an array. On a 32-bit system, each array element is likely to use 4 bytes. That means the RAM requirements for this data structure are approximately 1,000 x 1,000 x 4, or 4 million bytes—even before any data is stored in the table!

When you analyze typical complex spreadsheets, you find that they rarely contain data in all cells. A complex spreadsheet is usually sparsely populated, with blocks of data here and there and blank cells in between. An array-based data structure, such as DefaultTableModel, consumes space even for empty cells. A custom, sparse model would be more appropriate for our spreadsheet program. Listing 10-3 shows a model implemented for SheetMetal using a HashMap as the underlying storage mechanism.

```
public class SpreadsheetModel extends AbstractTableModel {
    public static int DEFAULT_ROW_COUNT = 1024;
    public static int DEFAULT_COLUMN_COUNT = 1024;

    private Map sparseMatrix = new HashMap();
    private int maxRow = 0;
    private int maxColumn = 0;

    private Point tmpIndex = new Point(0,0);

    public int getRowCount() {
        return DEFAULT_ROW_COUNT;
    }

    public int getColumnCount() {
        return DEFAULT_COLUMN_COUNT;
    }
    public Object getValueAt(int row, int column) {

        tmpIndex.y = row;
```

```
            tmpIndex.x = column;
            Object returnVal = sparseMatrix.get(tmpIndex);
            if (returnVal != null) {
               return returnVal;
            } else {
               return "";
            }
        }

        public void setValueAt(Object val, int row, int column) {
            if (val == null) {
                sparseMatrix.remove(new Point(column, row));
                return;
            }
            maxRow = Math.max(row, maxRow);
            maxColumn = Math.max(column, maxColumn);
            sparseMatrix.put(new Point(column, row), val);
        }

        public boolean isCellEditable( int row, int column ) {
            return true;
        }

        public int getMaxRow() {
            return maxRow;
        }

        public int getMaxColumn() {
            return maxColumn;
        }
    }
```

Listing 10-3   A sparse `TableModel`

The advantage of this custom data structure is that it starts out very small and grows as more data is added. Where the array-based structure uses several mega-bytes of memory when it's created, this one uses only about a kilobyte.

Although this structure is somewhat slower than an array-based structure, profiling shows that the overhead is only about 1 percent of the overall time it takes to render the table.

Obviously, it wouldn't make sense to always use a sparse model like this one. If the data is truly dense, the storage requirements for this type of structure are far greater than for the array-based structure. The point is to keep in mind that you have complete control over how your data is stored. Using a custom model can result in a large savings—and using the wrong model can carry a hefty penalty. This tactic isn't limited to `JTable`; you can use custom models with other controls as well.

10.2.5   Using Custom Renderers

Custom renderers are commonly created to control the appearance of a `JTable`, `JTree`, or `JList`. However, custom renderers can also sometimes be used to improve performance. Conversely, when implemented poorly, custom renderers can be highly detrimental to your program's performance. It's crucial that you understand the renderer mechanism so you can make the right implementation decisions.

As shown in Figure 10-4, each time a cell in a `JTable` is drawn, the data is fetched from the model and used to configure the renderer. The renderer is then used to draw the contents of the cell. The previous section mentions that it is common for spreadsheet data to be sparse—many cells are totally empty. Although the `DefaultTableCellRenderer` is smart enough not to draw anything for empty cells, there is still a lot of configuration and setup overhead for each cell. Since we know that the data for the SheetMetal application is sparse, we can write a custom renderer that is optimized for sparse data. This renderer is shown in Listing 10-4.

```
public class FastStringRenderer extends DefaultTableCellRenderer {

    Component stubRenderer = new NothingComponent();

    public Component getTableCellRendererComponent(JTable table,
                                                   Object value,
                                                   boolean isSelected,
                                                   boolean hasFocus,
                                                   int row,
                                                   int column) {

        if ( ((String)value).length() == 0 &&
             !isSelected && !has-Focus) {
          return stubRenderer;
        }

        return super.getTableCellRendererComponent(table, value,
                                                   isSelected,
                                                   hasFocus,
                                                   row, column);
    }

    class NothingComponent extends JComponent {
       public void paint(Graphics g) {
          // Do Nothing
       }
    }
}
```

Listing 10-4   Sparse data renderer

> ### getValueAt
>
> When creating your own models, keep in mind that the getValueAt method is called every time a cell is rendered. Neither the Component or Renderer cache the value; they request the data each time a cell needs to be updated. Since getValueAt is called so often, it has the potential to become a major bottleneck for your program.
>
> The Swing team once received a piece of code from a developer who was trying to figure out why his application was performing so poorly. It turned out that the developer's custom model performed complex matrix arithmetic inside its getValueAt method. This matrix computation calculated the state of the entire table, not just a single cell. Once the developer understood the model architecture, he was able to restructure his code to run much faster.

This sparse data renderer short-circuits the normal rendering process in two ways. First, it checks to see if the cell is empty (the string length is zero). Second, it checks to make sure that the cell isn't selected and doesn't have the focus. If the cell doesn't meet these conditions, the cell needs to be drawn and should be processed normally. To process the cell normally, the inherited version of getTableCellRendererComponent is called. This implementation sets up the component and returns the cell settings, such as its colors, borders, and other properties.

If the cell meets all of the conditions—the cell is totally empty, it isn't selected, and doesn't have the focus—all of the setup operations are bypassed and a NothingComponent is returned. Avoiding the setup costs eliminates numerous unnecessary method invocations.

The other optimization implemented in the fast renderer is that NothingComponent overrides the paint method so it doesn't do anything. Although the DefaultTableCellRenderer is smart enough to detect that the cell is empty and not draw anything, it still performs a considerable amount of setup and computation. By totally canceling out the call to paint, this unnecessary work is avoided.

Table 10-1 shows a spreadsheet's scrolling speed with the default renderer and with the sparse data renderer. Measurements for both renderers are shown with different amounts of data in the spreadsheet: empty, sparsely populated, and densely populated. The time is the number of milliseconds it took to scroll through 200 rows of the table.

As you can see, the results of this optimization are noticeable, but not dramatic. For a table of empty cells, the sparse data renderer is about 15 percent

Table State	Default Renderer	Sparse Data Renderer
Empty	1,150 ms	990 ms
1/3 full	1,150 ms	1,050 ms
Full	1,150 ms	1,200 ms

Table 10-1   Spreadsheet Scrolling Speed

faster. For a sparsely populated table (1/3 full), the fast renderer is about 10 percent faster. Notice, however, that when all of the cells in the table are full, the sparse data renderer is actually about 4 percent slower.

While this particular optimization isn't necessarily appropriate in all cases, it demonstrates that controlling the rendering process by implementing a custom renderer can be a worthwhile optimization. In your own programs, this tactic might open up opportunities for caching, short-circuiting, or other aggressive optimizations.

Rendering Component Objects

While custom renderers can improve performance, they can be a major problem if implemented incorrectly. One common mistake that we've seen several developers make can lead to poor performance or even cause a program to terminate with an `OutOfMemoryError`.

One of the main reasons that the renderer subsystem exists is that it would require too many resources to represent each table cell with a separate `Component`. This means that a `getTableCellRendererComponent` method should *not* create a new `Component` each time it is called.

Take another look at Listing 10-4. Note that a single instance of `NothingComponent` is created when the renderer is initialized. This instance is returned each time one is needed. `DefaultTableCellRenderer` actually inherits from `JLabel` and typically returns a reference to `this` each time a `Component` is needed for rendering.

The key is to reuse the same instance each time, changing only the configuration information each time you return it. Otherwise, you're likely to create thousands of `Component` objects, which can quickly swamp the garbage collector with megabytes of temporary objects.

10.2.6 Using Custom Models and Renderers Together

You don't need to choose between using a custom model and a custom renderer—both can be used in the same JComponent. The row header in the SheetMetal application provides an example of this. Swing provides an easy-to-use mechanism to label table columns, but doesn't provide one for rows. Fortunately, it is fairly easy to create one.

The simplest way to label rows is to create a new table to act as the row header. This JTable customizes both the model and the renderer. Listing 10-5 shows the SpreadsheetRowHeader used in SheetMetal. SpreadsheetRowHeader contains two inner classes: RowHeaderRenderer and RowHeaderModel.

```
public class SpreadsheetRowHeader extends JTable {
   TableCellRenderer render = new RowHeaderRenderer();

   public SpreadsheetRowHeader(JTable table) {
      super(new RowHeaderModel(table));
      configure(table);

   }
   protected void configure(JTable table) {
      setRowHeight(table.getRowHeight());
      setIntercellSpacing(new Dimension(0,0));
      setShowHorizontalLines(false);
      setShowVerticalLines(false);
   }

   public Dimension getPreferredScrollableViewportSize() {
      return new Dimension(32, super.getPreferredSize().height);
   }
   public TableCellRenderer getDefaultRenderer(Class c) {
      return render;
   }

   static class RowHeaderModel extends AbstractTableModel {
      JTable table;
      protected RowHeaderModel(JTable tableToMirror) {
         table = tableToMirror;
      }
      public int getRowCount() {
         return table.getModel().getRowCount();
      }
      public int getColumnCount() {
         return 1;
      }
      public Object getValueAt(int row, int column) {
         return String.valueOf(row+1);
      }
   }
}
   static class RowHeaderRenderer extends DefaultTableCellRenderer {
```

```
public Component getTableCellRendererComponent(JTable table,
                                                Object value,
                                                boolean isSelect,
                                                boolean hasFocus,
                                                int row,
                                                int column) {

    setBackground(UIManager.getColor("TableHeader.background"));
    setForeground(UIManager.getColor("TableHeader.foreground"));
    setBorder(UIManager.getBorder("TableHeader.cellBorder"));
    setFont(UIManager.getFont("TableHeader.font"));
    setValue(value);
    return this;
    }
  }
}
```

Listing 10-5   Table row header

RowHeaderRenderer is in charge of actually drawing the cells of the row
header. From a performance perspective, there's nothing particularly interesting
about the RowHeaderRenderer class. It simply configures itself to look like
Swing's built-in column headers by accessing values from the UIManager.

RowHeaderModel controls how the table data is stored. From a performance
perspective, the RowHeaderModel class is quite interesting. Since it's possible to
have literally millions of rows in a JTable, it would be nice if the row header's
storage requirements were not bound to the number of rows in the table. This is
exactly how RowHeaderModel works. As a result, it uses virtually no storage and
its RAM requirements don't grow with the number of rows in the table. The only
storage allocated by RowHeaderModel is a reference to the JTable that it is label-
ing. The RowHeaderModel getValueAt method simply converts the row number
passed to the method into a String—no long-term storage is allocated.

Key Points

- Swing's model-renderer architecture allows you to control how your data is stored and displayed. This is key to creating components that manipulate very large datasets.

- When changing data stored in models, perform the operations in bulk whenever possible. This reduces the number of events posted by the model.

- Use custom models to handle large datasets. The default models provided with Swing are generic and designed for light-duty use.

- Custom renderers can sometimes be used to improve performance.

- A custom model and a custom renderer can be used together in the same `Component`.

CHAPTER 11

Writing Responsive User Interfaces with Swing

MUCH of what has been written about GUI design focuses on the layout of controls, the presentation of data, and the mechanics of completing various tasks. However, even a program that has a great-looking, intuitive interface can be virtually unusable if it doesn't respond well to user actions. Performance is a key aspect of GUI design that's often overlooked until it's identified as a problem late in the development cycle.

This chapter provides a set of design guidelines and techniques you can use to ensure that your Swing GUIs perform well and provide fast, sensible responses to user input. Many of these guidelines imply the need for threads, and sections 11.2, 11.3, and 11.4 review the rules for using threads in Swing GUIs and the situations that warrant them. Section 11.5 describes a web-search application that illustrates how to apply these guidelines.

Note: Sections 11.2 and 11.3 are adapted from articles that were originally published on *The Swing Connection*. For more information about programming with Swing, visit *The Swing Connection* online at *http://java.sun.com/products/jfc/tsc/*.

11.1 Guidelines for Responsive GUIs

This section introduces two basic guidelines for writing responsive GUIs:

- Design, then build.
- Put the user in charge.

Following these guidelines should mitigate or eliminate GUI responsiveness problems. However, you need to consider the specific recommendations that follow in the context of your own program and apply the ones that make sense.

11.1.1   Design, Then Build (Repeat)

In nearly any engineering endeavor, it's important to spend time designing your product before you try to build it. While this is obvious, it's not always as clear how much time you should spend on the design before you start trying to implement it.

Design work tends to be time-consuming and expensive, while building software that implements a good design is relatively easy. To economize on the design part of the process, you need to have a good feel for how much refinement is really necessary.

For example, if you want to build a small program that displays the results of a simple fixed database query as a graph and in tabular form, there's probably no point in spending a week working out the best threading and painting strategies. To make this sort of judgment, you need to understand your program's scope and have a feel for how much it pushes the limits of the underlying technology.

To build a responsive GUI, you'll generally need to spend a little more time on certain aspects of your design:

- Managing component lifecycles. If you're working with a large number of GUI components, think carefully about how and when they're created. You also need to consider when to cache, reuse, and discard components.

- Constructing windows. If your GUI contains more than a handful of optional windows, construct and cache the windows that are most likely to be needed next. For example, in a forms application where a small subset of forms is shown to the user for a particular task, cache the forms that are relevant for that task.

- Handling timing issues in distributed applications. If your program uses services provided by other machines, or even other processes on the same machine, its GUI must accommodate performance latencies and other unpredictable timing issues. This is essential to making the program feel responsive to the user.

11.1.2   Put the User in Charge

Today, new programs are often distributed—they depend on services provided by other processes on a network, often the Internet. In this environment, a good performance model for a program is taking a dog for a walk: It's OK for the dog to stop and sniff as long as a tug on the leash gets a quick, appropriate response. Your program is the dog and the user is holding its leash. Your performance-engineering job is to make sure that the leash is as short as possible and your program is well-behaved. You don't want your 200-pound Labrador rolling around in the neighbor's geraniums on a 50-foot leash made of rubber bands.

The following sections describe four key guidelines for keeping your distributed applications in check:

- Don't make the user wait.
- Let the user know what's going on.
- Stay in sync.
- If it looks idle, it should be idle.

Don't Make the User Wait

If the user has to wait for more than 50 milliseconds for a response, the program is going to seem slow. Pauses of less than 50 milliseconds between when the user presses a key or button and when the GUI responds feel instantaneous to the user. As the delay grows, the GUI begins to feel sluggish. When the delay reaches 5 seconds or more, users are likely to assume that the program isn't working at all. In response, they often bash the keyboard and mouse in frustration, which can render the program truly nonfunctional.

In a distributed application, it's often not possible to provide results instantaneously. However, a well-designed GUI acknowledges the user's input immediately and shows results incrementally whenever possible.

Let the User Know What's Going On

When the user launches a time-consuming task and has to wait for the results, make it clear what's going on. If possible, give an estimate of how long it will take to complete the task. If you can't provide a reasonable estimate, say so.

Your interface should never be unresponsive to user input. Users should always be able to interrupt time-consuming tasks and get immediate feedback from the GUI.

Interrupting pending tasks safely and quickly can be a challenging design problem. In distributed systems, aborting a complex task can sometimes be as time-consuming as completing the task. In these cases, it's better to let the task complete and discard the results. The important thing is to immediately return the GUI to the state it was in before the task was started. If necessary, the program can continue the cleanup process in the background.

Stay in Sync

Distributed applications often display information that's stored on remote servers. You need to make sure that the displayed data stays in sync with the remote data.

One way to do this is to use explicit notifications. For example, if the information is part of the state of an Enterprise JavaBeans component, the program might add property change listeners for each of the properties being displayed. When one of the properties is changed, the program receives a notification and triggers a GUI update. However, this approach has scalability issues: You might receive more notifications than can be processed efficiently.

To avoid having to handle too many updates, you can insert a notification *concentrator* object between the GUI and the bean. The concentrator limits the number of updates that are actually sent to the GUI to one every 100 milliseconds or more. Another solution is to explicitly poll the state periodically—for example, once every 100 milliseconds.

If It Looks Idle, It Should Be Idle

When a program appears to be idle, it really should be idle. For example, when an application is iconified, it should remove listeners that have been installed on objects in other processes and pause or terminate polling threads. Conversely, if a program is consuming resources, there should be some evidence of that on the screen. This gets back to letting the user know what's going on. •

Imagine a program that displays the results of a database query each time the user presses a button. If the results don't change, the user might think that the program isn't working correctly. Although the program isn't idle (it is in fact performing the query), it looks idle. To fix this problem, you could display a status bar that contains the latest query and the time it was submitted, or display a transient highlight over the fields that are being updated even if the values don't change.

11.2   Using Threads in Swing Programs

The design guidelines presented in Section 11.1 lead to certain implementation decisions, particularly concerning the use of threads. Using threads properly can be the key to creating a responsive user interface with Swing. Because support for threads was built into the Java programming language, using threads is relatively easy; however, using them correctly can be difficult.

Event processing in Swing is effectively single-threaded, so you don't have to be well-versed in writing threaded applications to write basic Swing programs. The following sections describe the three rules you need to keep in mind when using threads in Swing:

- Swing components can be accessed by only one thread at a time. Generally, this thread is the event-dispatching thread. (A few operations are guaranteed to be thread-safe, notably `repaint` and `revalidate` methods on `JComponent`.)

- Use `invokeLater` and `invokeAndWait` for doing work if you need to access the GUI from outside event-handling or drawing code.

- If you need to create a thread, use a thread utility class such as `SwingWorker` or `Timer`. For example, you might want to create a thread to handle a job that's computationally expensive or I/O bound.

11.2.1   The Single-Thread Rule

Once a Swing component has been realized, all code that might affect or depend on the state of that component should be executed in the event-dispatching thread. This might sound scary, but for many simple programs, you don't have to worry about threads at all.

Realized means that the component's `paint` method has been or might be called. A Swing component that's a top-level window is realized by having `setVisible(true)`, `show`, or (this might surprise you) `pack` called on it. Once a window is realized, all of the components that it contains are realized. Another way to realize a `Component` is to add it to a `Container` that's already realized.

The *event-dispatching thread* is the thread that executes the drawing and event-handling code. For example, the `paint` and `actionPerformed` methods are automatically executed in the event-dispatching thread. Another way to execute code in the event-dispatching thread is to use the AWT `EventQueue.invokeLater` method.

There are a few exceptions to the single-thread rule:

- A few methods are thread-safe. In the Swing API documentation, thread-safe methods are tagged with the message: *"This method is thread safe, although most Swing methods are not."*

- A program's GUI can often be constructed and displayed in the main thread. (See the next section, Constructing a GUI in the Main Thread, for more information.)

- An applet's GUI can be constructed and displayed in its `init` method. Existing browsers don't render an applet until after its `init` and `start` methods have been called, so constructing the GUI in the applet's `init` method is safe as long as you never call `show` or `setVisible(true)` on the actual applet object.

- Three `JComponent` methods can be called from any thread: `repaint`, `revalidate`, and `invalidate`. The `repaint` and `revalidate` methods queue requests for the event-dispatching thread to call `paint` and `validate`, respectively. The `invalidate` method just marks a component and all of its direct ancestors as requiring validation.

- Listener lists can be modified from any thread. It's always safe to call the `add<ListenerType>Listener` and `remove<ListenerType>Listener` methods. These operations have no effect on event dispatches that might be under way.

Constructing a GUI in the Main Thread

You can safely construct and display a program's GUI in the `main` thread. For example, the code in Listing 11-1 is safe, as long as no `Component` objects (Swing or otherwise) have been realized.

```
public class MyApplication {
    public static void main(String[] args) {
        JPanel mainAppPanel = new JPanel();
        JFrame f = new JFrame("MyApplication");
        f.getContentPane().add(mainAppPanel,
                               BorderLayout.CENTER);
        f.pack();
        f.setVisible(true);
        // No more GUI work here
    }
}
```

Listing 11-1   Constructing a GUI in the `main` thread

In this example, the `f.pack` call realizes the components in the `JFrame`. According to the single-thread rule, the `f.setVisible(true)` call is unsafe and should be executed in the event-dispatching thread. However, as long as the program doesn't already have a visible GUI, it's exceedingly unlikely that the `JFrame` or its contents will receive a `paint` call before `f.setVisible(true)` returns. Because there's no GUI code after the `f.setVisible(true)` call, all GUI processing moves from the `main` thread to the event-dispatching thread, and the preceding code is thread-safe.

11.2.2   Using `invokeLater` and `invokeAndWait` for Event Dispatching

Most post-initialization GUI work naturally occurs in the event-dispatching thread. Once the GUI is visible, most programs are driven by events such as button actions or mouse clicks, which are always handled in the event-dispatching thread.

A program that uses separate worker threads to perform GUI-related processing can use invokeLater and invokeAndWait methods to cause a Runnable object to be run on the event-dispatching thread.

These methods were originally provided in the SwingUtilities class, but are part of the EventQueue class in the java.awt package in J2SE v. 1.2 and later. The SwingUtilities methods are now just wrappers for the AWT versions.

- invokeLater requests that some code be executed in the event-dispatching thread. This method returns immediately, without waiting for the code to execute.

- invokeAndWait acts like invokeLater, except that it waits for the code to execute. Generally, you should use invokeLater instead.

The two following sections show some examples of how these methods are used.

Using the invokeLater Method
You can call invokeLater from any thread to request the event-dispatching thread to run certain code. You must put this code in the run method of a Runnable object and specify the Runnable object as the argument to invokeLater. The invokeLater method returns immediately, it doesn't wait for the event-dispatching thread to execute the code. Listing 11-2 shows how to use invokeLater.

```
Runnable doWork = new Runnable() {
    public void run() {
        // do some GUI work here
    }
};
SwingUtilities.invokeLater(doWork);
```

Listing 11-2 Using invokeLater

Using the invokeAndWait Method
The invokeAndWait method is just like the invokeLater method, except that invokeAndWait doesn't return until the event-dispatching thread has executed the specified code. Whenever possible, you should use invokeLater instead of invokeAndWait. If you use invokeAndWait, make sure that the thread that calls invokeAndWait does not hold any locks that other threads might need while the invoked code is running. Listing 11-3 shows how to use invokeAndWait.

Listing 11-4 shows how a thread that needs access to GUI state, such as the contents of a pair of JTextFields, can use invokeAndWait to access the necessary information.

```
void showHelloThereDialog() throws Exception {
    Runnable doShowModalDialog = new Runnable() {
        public void run() {
            JOptionPane.showMessageDialog(myMainFrame,
                                          "HelloThere");
        }
    };
    SwingUtilities.invokeAndWait(doShowModalDialog);
}
```

Listing 11-3   Using `invokeAndWait`

```
void printTextField() throws Exception {
    final String[] myStrings = new String[2];

    Runnable doGetTextFieldText = new Runnable() {
        public void run() {
            myStrings[0] = textField0.getText();
            myStrings[1] = textField1.getText();
        }
    };
    SwingUtilities.invokeAndWait(doGetTextFieldText);

    System.out.println(myStrings[0] + " " + myStrings[1]);
}
```

Listing 11-4   Using `invokeAndWait` to access GUI state

Remember that you only need to use these methods if you want to update the GUI from a worker thread that you created. If you haven't created any threads, then you don't need to use `invokeLater` or `invokeAndWait`.

11.3   Using Timers in Swing Applications

Programs often need to schedule tasks to perform them repeatedly or perform them after a delay. An easy way to schedule tasks is to use a timer. As of J2SE v. 1.3, the Java platform provides two `Timer` classes: one in the `javax.swing` package and the other in `java.util`.

11.3.1   How Timers Work

Generally speaking, a timer enables a task to be executed either periodically or at a specific time. Timers are important, albeit specialized, tools for the GUI programmer because they simplify the job of scheduling activity that results in a screen update. GUI programs typically use timers for animation, such as for

Why Is Swing Implemented This Way?

There are several advantages to executing all of the user interface code in a single thread:

- *Component developers do not have to have an in-depth understanding of thread programming.* Toolkits like ViewPoint and Trestle, in which all components must fully support multithreaded access, can be difficult to extend, particularly for developers who are not expert at thread programming. Many of the toolkits developed more recently, such as SubArctic and IFC, have designs similar to Swing's.

- *Events are dispatched in a predictable order.* The runnable objects queued by `invokeLater` are dispatched from the same event queue as mouse and keyboard events, timer events, and paint requests. In toolkits where components support multithreaded access, component changes are interleaved with event processing at the whim of the thread scheduler. This makes comprehensive testing difficult or impossible.

- *Less overhead.* Toolkits that attempt to lock critical sections carefully can spend a substantial amount of time and space managing locks. Whenever the toolkit calls a method that might be implemented in client code (for example, any `public` or `protected` method in a `public` class), the toolkit must save its state and release all locks so that the client code can acquire locks if it needs to. When control returns from the method, the toolkit has to reacquire its locks and restore its state. All programs bear the cost of this, even though most programs do not require concurrent access to the GUI.

blinking a cursor, and for timing responses, such as displaying a tool tip when the mouse is still for a few moments.

Nearly every computer platform has a timer facility of some kind. For example, UNIX programs can use the `alarm` function to schedule a `SIGALRM` signal; a signal handler can then perform the task. The Win32 API has functions, such as `SetTimer`, that let you schedule and manage timer callbacks. The Java platform's timer facility includes the same basic functionality as other platforms, and it's relatively easy to configure and extend.

11.3.2   Code Without Timers

In programs written without timers, you'll see some rather nasty code for implementing delays and periodic task execution. The nastiest algorithm of all is the busy wait loop, shown in Listing 11-5. This little embarrassment attempts to create a delay by keeping the CPU busy, which is obviously a bad idea and likely to produce unpredictable results.

```
//DON'T DO THIS!
while (isCursorBlinking()) {
   drawCursor();
   for (int i = 0; i < 300000; i++) {
      Math.sqrt((double)i); // this should chew up time
   }
   eraseCursor();
   for (int i = 0; i < 300000; i++) {
      Math.sqrt((double)i); // likewise
   }
}
```

Listing 11-5   Busy wait loop

A more practical solution for implementing delays or timed loops is to create a new thread that sleeps before executing its task. Using the Thread sleep method to time a delay works well with Swing components as long as you follow the rules for thread usage outlined in Section 11.4 on page 176. The blinking cursor example could be rewritten using Thread.sleep, as shown in Listing 11-6. As you can see, the invokeLater method is used to ensure that the draw and erase methods execute on the event-dispatching thread.

```
final Runnable doUpdateCursor = new Runnable() {
   boolean shouldDraw = false;

   public void run() {
      if (shouldDraw = !shouldDraw) {
         drawCursor();
      } else {
         eraseCursor();
      }
   }
};

Runnable doBlinkCursor = new Runnable() {
   public void run() {
      while (isCursorBlinking()) {
         try {
            EventQueue.invokeLater(doUpdateCursor);
            Thread.sleep(300);
```

```
            } catch (InterruptedException e) {
               return;
            }
         }
      }
};
new Thread(doBlinkCursor).start();
```

Listing 11-6   Using the `Thread` `sleep` method

The main problem with this approach is that it doesn't scale well. Threads and thread scheduling aren't free or even as cheap as one might hope, so in a system where there might be many busy threads it's unwise to allocate a thread for every delay or timing loop.

11.3.3   The Swing `Timer` Class

The `javax.swing.Timer` class allows you to schedule an arbitrary number of periodic or delayed actions with just one thread. This `Timer` class is used by Swing components for things like blinking the text cursor and for timing the display of tool-tips.

The Swing timer implementation fires an action event whenever the specified interval or delay time passes. You need to provide an `Action` object to the timer. Implement the `Action` `actionPerformed` method to perform the desired task. For example, the blinking cursor example above could be written as shown in Listing 11-7. In this example, a timer is used to blink the cursor every 300 milliseconds.

```
Action updateCursorAction = new AbstractAction() {
   boolean shouldDraw = false;
   public void actionPerformed(ActionEvent e) {
      if (shouldDraw = !shouldDraw) {
         drawCursor();
      } else {
         eraseCursor();
      }
   }
};
new Timer(300, updateCursorAction).start();
```

Listing 11-7   Blinking cursor

The important difference between using the Swing `Timer` class and creating your own `Thread` is that the Swing `Timer` class uses just one thread for all timers. It deals with scheduling actions and putting its thread to sleep internally in a way that scales to large numbers of timers. The other important feature of this timer class is that the `Action` `actionPerformed` method runs on the event-dispatching thread. As a result, you don't have to bother with an explicit `invokeLater` call.

11.3.4   The Utility `Timer` and `TimerTask` Classes

Timers aren't the exclusive domain of GUI programs. In J2SE v. 1.3, support for timers was added to the `java.util` package. Like the Swing `Timer` class, the main `java.util` timer class is called `Timer`. (We'll call it the "utility `Timer` class" to differentiate from the Swing `Timer` class.) Instead of scheduling `Action` objects, the utility `Timer` class schedules instances of a class called `TimerTask`.

The utility timer facility has a different division of labor from the Swing version. For example, you control the utility timer facility by invoking methods on `TimerTask` rather than on `Timer`. Still, both timer facilities have the same basic support for delayed and periodic execution. The most important difference between `javax.Swing.Timer` and `java.util.Timer` is that the latter doesn't run its tasks on the event-dispatching thread.

The utility timer facility provides more flexibility over scheduling timers. For example, the utility timer lets you specify whether a timer task is to run at a fixed rate or repeatedly after a fixed delay. The latter scheme, which is the only one supported by Swing timers, means that a timer's frequency can drift because of extra delays introduced by the garbage collector or by long-running timer tasks. This drift is acceptable for animations or auto-repeating a keyboard key, but it's not appropriate for driving a clock or in situations where multiple timers must effectively be kept in lockstep.

The blinking cursor example can easily be implemented using the `java.util.Timer` class, as shown in Listing 11-8.

```
final Runnable doUpdateCursor = new Runnable() {
   private boolean shouldDraw = false;
   public void run() {
      if (shouldDraw = !shouldDraw) {
         drawCursor();
      } else {
         eraseCursor();
      }
   }
};
TimerTask updateCursorTask = new TimerTask() {
   public void run() {
      EventQueue.invokeLater(doUpdateCursor);
   }
};
myGlobalTimer.schedule(updateCursorTask, 0, 300);
```

Listing 11-8   Blinking the cursor with `java.util.Timer`

An important difference to note when using the utility `Timer` class is that each `java.util.Timer` instance, such as `myGlobalTimer`, corresponds to a single thread. It's up to the program to manage the `Timer` objects.

11.3.5   How to Choose a Timer Class

As we've seen, the Swing and utility timer facilities provide roughly the same functionality. Generally speaking, we recommend that you use the utility classes if you're writing a self-contained program, particularly one that's not GUI-related. The Swing `Timer` class is preferred if you're building a new Swing component or module that doesn't require large numbers of timers (where "large" means dozens or more).

The new utility timer classes give you control over how many timer threads are created; each `java.util.Timer` object creates one thread. If your program requires large numbers of timers you might want to create several `java.util.Timer` objects and have each one schedule related `TimerTasks`. In a typical program you'll share just one global `Timer` object, for which you'll need to create one statically scoped `Timer` field or property.

The Swing `Timer` class uses a single private thread to schedule timers. A typical GUI component or program uses at most a handful of timers to control various animation and pop-up effects. The single thread is more than sufficient for this.

The other important difference between the two facilities is that Swing timers run their task on the event-dispatching thread, while utility timers do not. You can hide this difference with a `TimerTask` subclass that takes care of calling `invokeLater`. Listing 11-9 shows a `TimerTask` subclass, `SwingTimerTask`, that does this. To implement the task, you would then subclass `SwingTimerTask` and override its doRun method (instead of `run`).

```
abstract class SwingTimerTask extends java.util.TimerTask {
    public abstract void doRun();
    public void run() {
        if (!EventQueue.isDispatchThread()) {
            EventQueue.invokeLater(this);
        } else {
            doRun();
        }
    }
}
```

Listing 11-9   Extending `TimerTask`

11.3.6   Timer Example

This example demonstrates an interesting use of timers. It displays an image and performs an animated cross-fade on the image when the user clicks a button. Selected frames of the animation are shown in Figure 11-1.

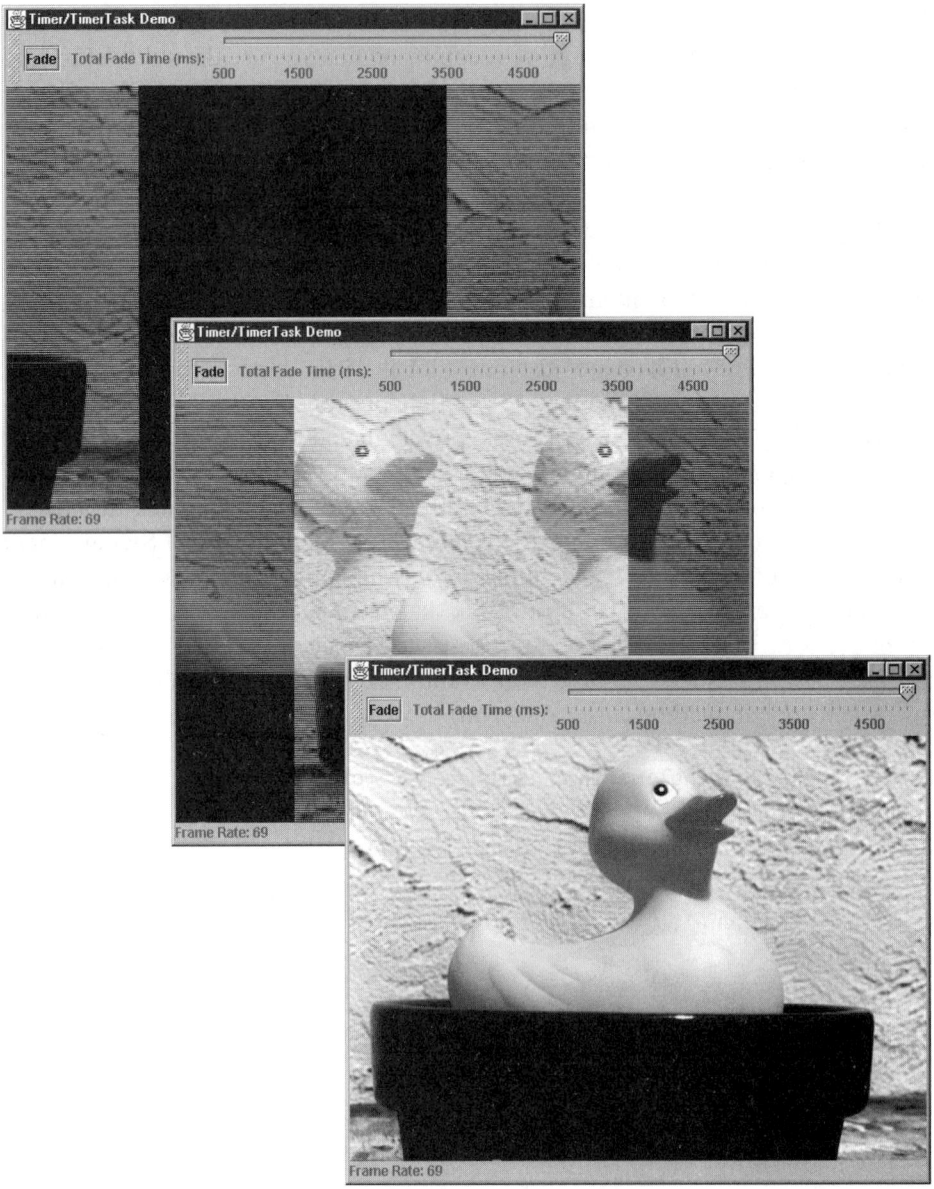

Figure 11-1   Cross-fade animation

This animation is implemented using the `java.util.Timer` and `SwingTimerTask` classes. The cross-fade is implemented using the `Graphics` and `Image` classes. Complete code for this sample is available online,[1] but this discussion concentrates on how the timers are used.

A `SwingTimerTask` is used to schedule the repaints for the animation. The actual fade operation is handled in the `paintComponent` method, which computes how far along the fade is supposed to be based on the current time, and paints accordingly.

The user interface provides a slider that lets the user control how long the fade takes—the shorter the time, the faster the fade. When the user clicks the Fade button, the setting from the slider is passed to the `startFade` method, shown in Listing 11-10. This method creates an anonymous subclass of `SwingTimerTask` (Listing 11-9) that repeatedly calls `repaint`. When the task has run for the allotted time, the task cancels itself.

```
public void startFade(long totalFadeTime) {

    SwingTimerTask updatePanTask = new SwingTimerTask() {
        public void doRun() {
            /* If we've used up the available time then cancel
             * the timer.
             */
            if ((System.currentTimeMillis()-startTime) >= totalTime) {
                endFade();
                cancel();
            }
        repaint();
        }
    };

    totalTime = totalFadeTime;
    startTime = System.currentTimeMillis();

    timer.schedule(updatePanTask, 0, frameRate);
}
```

Listing 11-10   Starting the animation

The last thing the `startFade` method does is schedule the task. The `schedule` method takes three arguments: the task to be scheduled, the delay before starting, and the number of milliseconds between calls to the task.

---

1. You can download the code for this and other examples from *http://java.sun.com/docs/books/performance/*.

It's usually easy to determine what value to use for the task delay. For example, if you want the cursor to blink five times every second, you set the delay to 200 milliseconds. In this case, however, we want to call repaint as often as possible so that the animation runs smoothly. If repaint is called too often, though, it's possible to swamp the CPU and fill the event queue with repaint requests faster than the requests can be processed. To avoid this problem, we calculate a reasonable frame rate and pass it to the schedule method as the task delay. This frame rate is calculated in the initFrameRate method shown in Listing 11-11.

```
public void initFrameRate() {
    Graphics g = createImage(imageWidth,
                                imageHeight).getGraphics();
    long dt = 0;
    for (int i = 0; i < 20; i++) {
        long startTime = System.currentTimeMillis();
        paintComponent(g);
        dt += System.currentTimeMillis() - startTime;
    }
    setFrameRate((long)((float)(dt / 20) * 1.1f));
}
```

Listing 11-11   Initializing the frame rate

The frame rate is calculated using the average time that it takes the paintComponent method to render the component to an offscreen image. The average time is multiplied by a factor of 1.1 to slow the frame rate by 10 percent to prevent minor fluctuations in drawing time from affecting the smoothness of the animation.

For additional information about using Swing timers, see How to Use Timers in *The Java Tutorial*.[2]

11.4   Responsive Applications Use Threads

Although threads need to be used carefully, using threads is often essential to making a Swing program responsive. If the user-centric guidelines presented in Section 11.1 were distilled down to their developer-centric essence, the rule for handling user-initiated tasks would be:

If it might take a long time or it might block, use a thread. If it can occur later or it should occur periodically, use a timer.

2. Mary Campione and Kathy Walrath, *The Java Tutorial: Object-Oriented Programming for the Internet, Second Edition*. Addison-Wesley, 1998.

Occasionally, it makes sense to create and start a thread directly; however, it's usually simpler and safer to use a robust thread-based utility class. A thread-based utility class is a more specialized, higher-level abstraction that manages a worker thread. The timer classes described in Section 11.3 are good examples of this type of utility class. *Concurrent Programming in Java*[3] by Doug Lea describes many other useful thread-based abstractions.

Swing provides a simple utility class called SwingWorker that can be used to perform work on a new thread and then update the GUI on the event-dispatching thread. SwingWorker is an abstract class. To use it, override the construct method to perform the work on a new thread. The SwingWorker finished method runs on the event-dispatching thread. Typically, you override finished to update the GUI based on the value produced by the construct method. (You can read more about the SwingWorker class on *The Swing Connection*.[4])

The example in Listing 11-12 shows how SwingWorker can be used to check the modified date of a file on an HTTP server. This is a sensible task to delegate to a worker thread because it can take a while and usually spends most of its time blocked on network I/O.

```
final JLabel label = new JLabel("Working ...");

SwingWorker worker = new SwingWorker() {
    public Object construct() {
        try {
            URL url = new URL("http://java.sun.com/index.html");
            return new Date(url.openConnection().getLastModified());
        }
        catch (Exception e) {
            return "";
        }
    }
    public void finished() {
        label.setText(get().toString());
    }
};
worker.start();  // start the worker thread
```

Listing 11-12   Checking the state of a remote file using a worker thread

In this example, the construct method returns the last-modified date for java.sun.com, or an error string if something goes wrong. The finished method

3. Doug Lea, *Concurrent Programming in Java: Design Principles and Patterns, Second Edition.* Addison-Wesley, 1999.

4. Visit *The Swing Connection* online at *http://java.sun.com/products/jfc/tsc/.*

uses `SwingWorker.get`, which returns the value computed by the `construct` method, to update the label's text.

Using a worker thread to handle a task like the one in the previous example does keep the event-dispatching thread free to handle user events; however, it doesn't magically transform your computer into a multi-CPU parallel-processing machine. If the task keeps the worker thread moderately busy, it's likely that the thread will absorb cycles that would otherwise be used by the event-dispatching thread and your program's on-screen performance will suffer. There are several ways to mitigate this effect:

- Keep the priority of worker threads low.

- Keep the number of worker threads small.

- Consider suspending worker threads during CPU-intensive operations like scrolling.

The example in the next section illustrates as many of these guidelines and techniques as possible. It's a front end for web search engines that resembles Apple's Sherlock 2 application[5] or (to a lesser extent) Infoseek's Express Search application.[6]

11.5   Example: Searching the Web

Some of the most popular web sites are the search engine portals like Yahoo! and AltaVista. The user interfaces for these web sites provide the results for a web search query in bundles of 10 to 20 query hits. To review more than the first bundle, the user clicks on a link that exposes another bundle. This can go on ad infinitum; queries often produce thousands of hits.

These types of user interfaces push the limit of what works well in the HTML-based, thin-client application model. Many of the operations that you might expect to find in a search program, such as sorting and filtering, can't easily be provided under this dumb-terminal-style application model.

On the other hand, the Java platform is uniquely suited for creating user interfaces for web services like search engines. The combination of networking libraries, HTTP libraries, language-level support for threads, and a comprehensive graphics and GUI toolkit make it possible to quickly create full-featured web-based applications.

---

5. For more information about Sherlock, see *http://www.apple.com/sherlock/.*

6. For more information about Express Search, see *http://express.go.com/.*

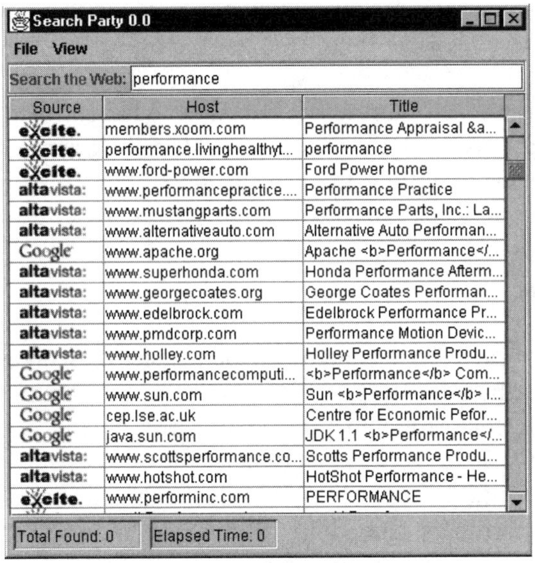

Figure 11-2   Search Party application

The Search Party application, shown in Figure 11-2, provides this kind of Java technology-based user interface for a set of web search engines. It illustrates how to apply the guidelines and techniques described in this chapter to create a responsive GUI. You can download the complete source code for the Search Party application from *http://java.sun.com/docs/books/performance/*.

Search Party allows the user to enter a simple query that's delivered to a list of popular search engines. The results are collected in a single table that can be sorted, filtered, and searched. The GUI keeps the user up-to-date on the search tasks that are running and lets the user interrupt a search at any time.

Worker threads are used to connect to the search engines and parse their results. Each worker thread delivers updates to the GUI at regular intervals. After collecting a couple hundred search hits, the worker thread exits. If the user interrupts the search, the worker threads are terminated.

The following sections take a closer look at how the worker threads operate.

11.5.1   Worker Thread Priority

Worker threads in the Search Party application are run at the lowest possible priority, `Thread.MIN_PRIORITY`. The thread-priority property allows you to advise the underlying system about the importance of scheduling the thread. How the thread-priority property is used depends on the JVM implementation. Some implementations make rather limited use of the priority property and small changes in thread priority have little or no effect. In other JVM implementations, a thread with a low priority might starve (never be scheduled) if there are always higher-priority threads that are ready to run.

In the Search Party application, the only thread we're concerned about competing with is the event-dispatching thread. Making the worker threads' priorities low is reasonable because we're always willing to suspend the worker threads while the user is interacting with the program.

11.5.2   Interrupting a Worker Thread

When the user presses the Search Party Stop button, all of the active worker threads are interrupted. The worker threads interpret the interrupt as a request to terminate: They close the network connection they're reading from, send any pending GUI updates to the event dispatching thread, and then exit.

When the Thread.interrupt method is called, it just sets the thread's interrupted boolean property. If the interrupted thread is sleeping or waiting, an InterruptedException is thrown. If the interrupted thread is blocked on I/O, an InterruptedIOException might be thrown, but throwing the exception isn't required by the JVM specification and most implementations don't.

Search Party's SwingWorker subclass, SearchWorker, checks to see if it's been interrupted each time it reads a character from the buffered input stream. Although the obvious way to implement this would be to call Thread.isInterrupted before reading a character, this approach isn't reliable. The isInterrupted flag is cleared when an InterruptedException is caught or when the special "interrupted" test and reset method is called. If some code that we've implicitly called happens to catch the InterruptedException (because it was waiting or sleeping) or if it clears the isInterrupted flag by calling Thread.interrupted, Search Party wouldn't realize that it's been interrupted! To make sure that Search Party detects interruptions, the SwingWorker interrupt method interrupts the worker thread and permanently sets the boolean flag that is returned by the SwingWorker method isInterrupted.

What happens if the interrupted worker thread is blocked on I/O while waiting for data from the HTTP server it's reading from? It's unlikely that the I/O code will throw an InterruptedIOException, which means there's a potential thread leak. To avoid this problem, SearchWorker class overloads the interrupt method. When the worker is interrupted, the input stream it's reading from is immediately closed. This has the nice side effect of immediately aborting any pending I/O. The SearchWorker implementation catches and ignores the I/O exception that results from closing the thread's input stream while a read was pending.

Key Points

- Using threads is essential for building responsive GUIs. Blocking user activity to wait for long tasks to complete leads to poor perceived performance.

- The user is the boss. Always let your users know what's going on and give them regular status updates when waiting for long tasks to complete.

- Once realized, Swing components should only be touched by code executing inside the AWT event-dispatch thread.

- Use `invokeLater` and `invokeAndWait` to move work to the event dispatching thread.

- Use timers for repeated operations. You can use either the `javax.swing.Timer` or `java.util.Timer`. The utility `Timer` class gives you more control, but you have to move work to the event-dispatch thread yourself. You can use the `SwingTimerTask` utility described in this chapter to move work to the event-dispatch thread.

- Use `SwingWorker` to execute time-consuming tasks on new threads and update the GUI on the event-dispatch thread.

- Interrupt worker threads when the user is driving the system.

CHAPTER 12

Deployment

DEPLOYMENT is a critical part of the development of your program. Choices you make about deployment may have little or no effect on your code, but can have a large impact on the perceived performance of your product. Your deployment choices are especially important for network-based applets and applications. The speed at which your program is downloaded and displayed is important to users, and can be very dependent on your deployment strategy.

This chapter discusses several ways to reduce the download time of network-based (intranet and Internet) applications, including the use of `javac` compiler options, Java Archive (JAR) files, commercial packaging utilities, and more.

12.1   Compiler Options

One fairly easy way to reduce download size of your program is to use the `javac -g:none` option when compiling the final version of your program. This strips all debugging information from the class files. Running a quick test with the Metalworks JFC demo (included in the SDK) shows about a 13 percent reduction in class file size by using this option, as shown in Table 12-1. Using the `-g:none` option also results in a slight reduction in RAM footprint.

The downside is that if your customers experience problems in the field, the problems can be slightly harder to debug. For example, stack traces from exceptions won't contain line numbers.

`javac *.java`	`javac -g:none*.java`
46K	40K

Table 12-1   Total Size of Class Files

12.2   JAR Files

JDK 1.1 introduced the concept of a JAR file. JAR files condense a number of class files (and other resources like GIF files) into one simple-to-deploy package. The JAR file format is based on the popular zip algorithm and provides compression as well as convenience. Putting your classes and resources into a JAR file can considerably decrease the overall number of bytes clients need to download in order to use your application. JAR files can also improve the start-up speed of applets downloaded from web servers by a far larger amount than the reduction in download size would imply.

12.2.1   Reducing Program Size

Table 12-2 shows the savings when the Metalworks JFC demo is saved in a JAR file. The complete uncompressed, unoptimized demo (both classes and resources) occupies 61K. When it's built without debug information, the size shrinks slightly to 55K. By putting these classes and resources in a JAR file, you get an even greater reduction in program size.

   The Uncompressed Size row contains the sum of the Class File Size and the Resource Size values. The JAR Size row is the size of the compressed JAR, which includes both the classes and resources. As you can see, removing the debug information and saving the program in a JAR file results in about a 38 percent reduction in the number of bytes downloaded to run this program.

	`javac *.java`	`javac -g:none *.java`
Class File Size	46K	40K
Resource Size	15K	15K
Uncompressed Size	61K	55K
JAR Size	42K	38K

Table 12-2   JAR File Sizes

12.2.2   Download Time Reduction

The benefits of JAR files go beyond just reducing the number of bytes that have to be downloaded to run your program. A major problem for web-deployed applets has to do with inefficiencies in the HTTP protocol. Clients connected to HTTP servers can generally download large files fairly quickly. However, HTTP is a poor protocol for downloading a lot of small files. Each file request sent to the server incurs additional overhead. If you put your program on a web server as a raw collection of classes and resources, a client downloading the program has to make a separate request for each file. This can be very slow for the client and increases the load on your web server.

To demonstrate the effectiveness of JAR files, the SwingSet demo applet was rebuilt and deployed two ways. First, all of the individual classes and resources were loaded into directories on a web server. Second, all the classes and resources were packed into single JAR file. Table 12-3 shows start-up times for several runs of the applet. For this test, a PC client was used to download the applet from a Solaris server running Apache web server on a 10base-T LAN. The times were measured with a stopwatch.

When the applet is deployed with a JAR file, the start-up time is more than six times faster. The improvement is even more pronounced in the worst-case scenario. These results are representative of the improvements in download times that result from using JAR files. As always, however, the results can vary widely depending on the particular circumstances.

Run Number	Separate Files	JAR File
1	69.75 seconds	8.87 seconds
2	57.75 seconds	8.89 seconds
3	51.09 seconds	9.68 seconds
4	54.72 seconds	9.21 seconds
5	89.16 seconds	9.50 seconds
6	51.50 seconds	9.78 seconds
7	56.35 seconds	9.28 seconds
Average	61.47 seconds	9.32 seconds
Best	51.09 seconds	8.87 seconds
Worst	89.16 seconds	9.78 seconds

Table 12-3   SwingSet Start-up Time

12.2.3   JAR Files and Resources

Converting an applet or application to run inside a JAR file is generally trivial—most of the time, no code changes are required. One case, however, is a common source of confusion: accessing files in the JAR file. When a file is *not* in a JAR file it can be accessed like this:

```
InputStream in = new FileInputStream("MyFile.txt");
```

However, if MyFile.txt is contained in a JAR file along with the class trying to access it, this code doesn't work. There is no longer a stand-alone file with the specified name; it's simply an entry in the larger compressed file.

To get around this problem, you need to use the Class.getResource and Class.getResourceAsStream methods. For example, to access the contents of MyFile.txt, you could use the following code:

```
InputStream in = this.getClass().getResourceAsStream("MyFile.txt");
```

See the documentation for Class for more information about the getResource methods.

12.3   Packaging Utilities

There are several commercial tools available that specialize in application and applet packaging. These tools typically provide you with the benefits of standard JAR files, but also claim several additional benefits. These generally include some or all of the following:

- Removal of unused code
- Code compression/obfuscation
- Reduced RAM footprint
- Faster runtime performance

Generally, these tools work by analyzing your class files and stripping dead code in a fashion similar to a traditional linker tool. They also modify the class files and shorten the names of fields and methods. For example, a method called getCustomerAddress might be shortened to simply a. This reduces the size of the class files and the JVM constants pool at runtime. There are many reports of developers getting 30 to 70 percent reductions in program size by using these packaging tools. Using a packaging tool can also reduce RAM footprint, though the reductions are usually fairly small.

Before deciding whether to use a packaging tool, be aware that some of these techniques are difficult for an automated tool to perform in a system that supports reflection and dynamic class loading, as the Java language does. For example, if the tool changes the name of a method that you try to look up with reflection, your lookup will fail. Some of the commercial tools have mechanisms to help you deal with this, but they often require manual intervention.

Another consideration is that the obfuscation of your code can make field debugging more difficult. For example, stack traces are often very useful in isolating bugs. After compression/obfuscation by one of these tools, however, the stack trace might no longer contain the original method names.

The claims that some tools make about improving program execution speed typically apply to code running in an interpreted environment. The techniques applied by these tools are much less compelling in an environment with a JIT—all of the speed optimizations available to static packaging tools are also available to JIT systems. Today's code generators currently implement many of these optimizations, and more and more of these optimizations will be implemented in the future. Obfuscators can actually make it harder for JITs to figure out how to generate optimal code, so it's important to consider your target environment when deciding whether or not to use a packaging tool.

Overall, packaging tools are useful in certain situations, particularly if you are very concerned about application size. You should evaluate these tools with your own code and develop benchmarks for the performance aspects that are important to you. When evaluating the results, keep the concerns related to reflection and dynamic class loading in mind—even if you aren't using these features right now, you might want to in the future. Before making any final decisions, discuss these issues and any other concerns you have with the product vendor.

12.4 Dynamic Downloading

A disadvantage of the JAR file format is that you have to download the entire JAR file before any of the classes it contains can be loaded. Even if only ten classes have to be downloaded before your applet's initial screen can be displayed, the client still has to wait for the entire applet to download before the program can start. As discussed earlier, the HTTP protocol is poor for downloading a lot of small class files, so just putting all of the individual files on the web server instead of in a JAR file doesn't really help. To address this problem, commercial products have recently been developed to support more dynamic downloading.

These dynamic downloading products generally require that you run a separate custom server process on the same machine as your web server. When a client requests your applet, a specially constructed small applet class is downloaded instead. This applet class, called a stub, then downloads the rest of your classes by making a connection (using a custom protocol) to the custom server process. This process is illustrated in Figure 12-1. Since the class file server doesn't have to use the HTTP protocol, it can download the classes much more efficiently. This type of system can also download classes in the background while the user performs other tasks.

While systems like this are new, they do show promise. The main drawback is that they require an additional process to be run on the web server, which is not practical in all environments. If the custom process can be run in your deployment environment, however, you might want to consider this option to maximize start-up performance.

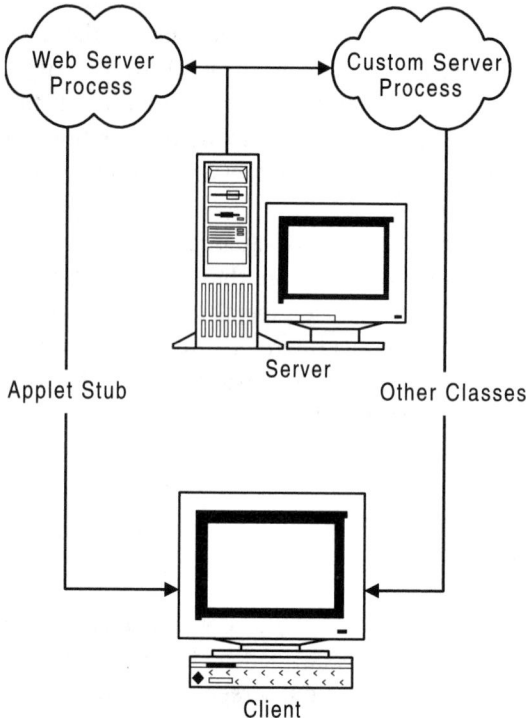

Figure 12-1   Dynamic class loader configuration

12.4.1   Applet Caching

Newer versions of Sun's Java Plug-in (starting with version 1.3) cache down-loaded applet JAR files. The first time an applet is run, it is downloaded normally. On subsequent runs, however, the applet loads with the same speed as if it were installed locally. This is an excellent option for applets that will be used by clients on a regular basis.

Key Points

- Although deployment choices might not affect your code, they can have a big impact on perceived performance.
- You can control whether debugging information is included in your class files. Removing debugging information can make your class files smaller.
- JAR files provide compression and are more efficient to download from web servers.
- Commercial packaging tools can be useful, but there can be issues with dynamic class loading, reflection, and debugging. Carefully evaluate any product before putting it into production use.

Appendices

THESE appendices provide information about garbage collection and the HotSpot virtual machine and how they can impact the performance of your Java programs.

Appendix A, The Truth About Garbage Collection (page 193)
To make intelligent choices about memory management issues, you need to have a basic understanding of how garbage collection works. This appendix provides an overview of the garbage collection mechanism and provides tips for handling memory in your Java programs.

Appendix B, The Java HotSpot Virtual Machine (page 205)
The Java HotSpot virtual machine uses cutting-edge techniques for memory management, thread synchronization, and dynamic compilation that can dramatically improve the performance of Java programs. This appendix provides an overview of the Hotspot VM and describes option settings that you can use to control the behavior of the Hotspot VM at runtime.

The Truth About Garbage Collection

GARBAGE collection (GC) is probably the most widely misunderstood feature of the Java platform. GC is typically advertised as removing all memory management responsibility from the application developer. This just isn't the case. On the other hand, some developers bend over backwards trying to please the collector, and often wind up doing much more work than is required. A solid understanding of the garbage collection model is essential to writing robust, high-performance software for the Java platform.

This appendix provides an overview of the garbage collection mechanisms that will help you make intelligent choices about memory management issues. It also contains information to help you debug complex problems such as memory leaks.

A.1   Why Should You Care About Garbage Collection?

The cost of allocating and collecting memory can play a significant role in how your software performs. The overall memory requirements of your software can have a huge impact on the speed of your program when large RAM requirements force the OS to use virtual memory. This often occurs when memory is allocated, but not properly released. Although the JVM is responsible for freeing unused memory, you have to make it clear what is unused. To write successful, large-scale programs, you need to understand the basics of the GC mechanism.

A.2   The Guarantees of GC

The specification for the Java platform makes very few promises about how garbage collection actually works. Here is what the *Java Virtual Machine Specification* (JVMS) has to say about memory management.

The heap is created on virtual machine start-up. Heap storage for objects is reclaimed by an automatic storage management system (known as a garbage collector); objects are never explicitly deallocated. The Java virtual machine assumes no particular type of automatic storage management system, and the storage management technique may be chosen according to the implementor's system requirements.[1]

While it can seem confusing, the fact that the garbage collection model is not rigidly defined is actually important and useful—a rigidly defined garbage collection model might be impossible to implement on all platforms. Similarly, it might preclude useful optimizations and hurt the performance of the platform in the long term.

Although there is no one place that contains a full definition of required garbage collector behavior, much of the GC model is implicitly specified through a number of sections in the *Java Language Specification* and JVMS. While there are no guarantees about the exact process followed, all compliant virtual machines share the basic object lifecycle described in this chapter.

A.3   The Object Lifecycle

In order to discuss garbage collection, it is first useful to examine the object lifecycle. An object typically goes through most of the following states between the time it is allocated and the time its resources are finally returned to the system for reuse.

1. Created

2. In use (strongly reachable)

3. Invisible

4. Unreachable

5. Collected

6. Finalized

7. Deallocated

---

1. Tim Lindholm and Frank Yellin, *The Java Virtual Machine Specification, Second Edition*, Section 3.5.3. Addison-Wesley, 1999.

A.3.1   Created

When an object is created, several things occur:[2]

1. Space is allocated for the object.

2. Object construction begins.

3. The superclass constructor is called.

4. Instance initializers and instance variable initializers are run.

5. The rest of constructor body is executed.

The exact costs of these operations depend on the implementation of the JVM, as well as the implementation of the class being constructed. The thing to keep in mind is that these costs exist. Once the object has been created, assuming it is assigned to some variable, it moves directly to the in use state.

A.3.2   In Use

Objects that are held by at least one strong reference are considered to be *in use*. In JDK 1.1.x, all references are strong references. Java 2 introduces three other kinds of references: weak, soft and phantom. (These reference types are discussed in Section A.4.1.) The example shown in Listing A-1 creates an object and assigns it to some variables.

```
public class CatTest {
        static Vector catList = new Vector();
        static void makeCat() {
                Object cat = new Cat();
                catList.addElement(cat);
        }

        public static void main(String[] arg) {
                makeCat();
                // do more stuff
        }
}
```

Listing A-1   Creating and referencing an object

Figure A-1 shows the structure of the objects inside the VM just before the makeCat method returns. At that moment, two strong references point to the Cat object.

---

2. James Gosling, Bill Joy, and Guy Steele, *The Java Language Specification, Second Edition.* Addison-Wesley, 2000.

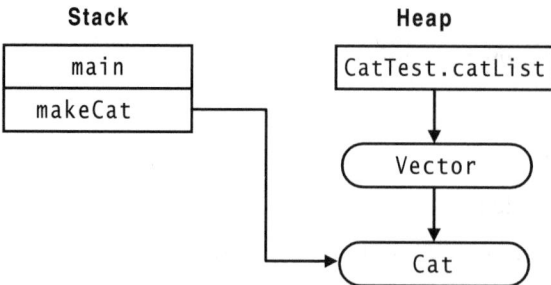

Figure A-1   Object reference graph

When the `makeCat` method returns, the stack frame for that method and any temporary variables it declares are removed. This leaves the `Cat` object with just a single reference from the `catList` static variable (indirectly via the `Vector`).

A.3.3   Invisible

An object is in the *invisible* state when there are no longer any strong references that are accessible to the program, even though there might still be references. Not all objects go through this state, and it has been a source of confusion for some developers. Listing A-2 shows a code fragment that creates an invisible object.

```
public void run() {
    try {
        Object foo = new Object();
        foo.doSomething();
    } catch (Exception e) {
        // whatever
    }
    while (true) { // do stuff } // loop forever
}
```

Listing A-2   Invisible object

In this example, the object `foo` falls out of scope when the `try` block finishes. It might seem that the `foo` temporary reference variable would be pulled off the stack at this point and the associated object would become unreachable. After all, once the `try` block finishes, there is no syntax defined that would allow the program to access the object again. However, an efficient implementation of the JVM is unlikely to zero the reference when it goes out of scope. The object referenced by `foo` continues to be strongly referenced, at least until the `run` method returns. In this case, that might not happen for a long time. Because invisible objects can't be collected, this is a possible cause of memory leaks. If you run into this situation, you might have to explicitly null your references to enable garbage collection.

A.3.4   Unreachable

An object enters an *unreachable* state when no more strong references to it exist. When an object is unreachable, it is a *candidate* for collection. Note the wording: Just because an object is a candidate for collection doesn't mean it will be immediately collected. The JVM is free to delay collection until there is an immediate need for the memory being consumed by the object.

It's important to note that not just any strong reference will hold an object in memory. These must be references that chain from a garbage collection root. GC roots are a special class of variable that includes

- Temporary variables on the stack (of any thread)
- Static variables (from any class)
- Special references from JNI native code

Circular strong references don't necessarily cause memory leaks. Consider the code in Listing A-3. It creates two objects, and assigns them references to each other.

```
public void buidDog() {
    Dog newDog = new Dog();
    Tail newTail = new Tail();
    newDog.tail = newTail;
    newTail.dog = newDog;
}
```

Listing A-3   Circular reference

Figure A-2 shows the reference graph for the objects before the `buildDog` method returns. Before the method returns, there are strong references from the temporary stack variables in the `buildDog` method pointing to both the `Dog` and the `Tail`.

Figure A-3 shows the graph for the objects after the `buildDog` method returns. At this point, the `Dog` and `Tail` both become unreachable from a root and are candidates for collection (although the VM might not actually collect these objects for an indefinite amount of time).

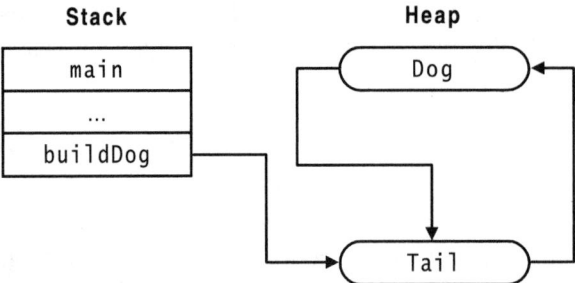

Figure A-2   Reference graph before buildDog returns

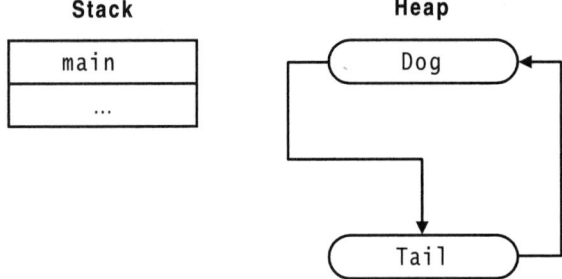

Figure A-3   Reference graph after buildDog returns

A.3.5   Collected

An object is in the *collected* state when the garbage collector has recognized an object as unreachable and readies it for final processing as a precursor to deallocation. If the object has a finalize method, then it is marked for finalization. If it does not have a finalizer then it moves straight to the finalized state.

If a class defines a finalizer, then any instance of that class must have the finalizer called prior to deallocation. This means that deallocation is delayed by the inclusion of a finalizer.

A.3.6   Finalized

An object is in the *finalized* state if it is still unreachable after its finalize method, if any, has been run. A finalized object is awaiting deallocation. Note that the VM implementation controls when the finalizer is run. The only thing that can be said for certain is that adding a finalizer will extend the lifetime of an object. This means that adding finalizers to objects that you intend to be short-lived is a bad idea. You are almost always better off doing your own cleanup instead of relying on a finalizer. Using a finalizer can also leave behind critical resources that won't be recovered for an indeterminate amount of time. If you are considering using a finalizer to ensure that important resources are freed in a timely manner, you might want to reconsider.

One case where a `finalize` method delayed GC was discovered by the quality assurance (QA) team working on Swing. The QA team created a stress testing application that simulated user input by using a thread to send artificial events to the GUI. Running on one version of the toolkit, the application reported an `OutOfMemoryError` after just a few minutes of testing. The problem was finally traced back to the fact that the thread sending the events was running at a higher priority than the finalizer thread. The program ran out of memory because about 10,000 `Graphics` objects were held in the finalizer queue waiting for a chance to run their finalizers. It turned out that these `Graphics` objects were holding onto fairly substantial native resources. The problem was fixed by assuring that whenever Swing is done with a `Graphics` object, `dispose` is called to ensure that the native resources are freed as soon as possible.

In addition to lengthening object lifetimes, finalize methods can increase object size. For example, some JVMs, such as the classic JVM implementation, add an extra hidden field to objects with `finalize` methods so that they can be held in a linked list finalization queue.

A.3.7   Deallocated

The deallocated state is the final step in garbage collection. If an object is still unreachable after all the above work has occurred, then it is a candidate for deallocation. Again, when and how deallocation occurs is up to the JVM.

A.4   Reference Objects

Prior to the introduction of the Java 2 platform, all references were strong references. This meant that there was no way for the developer to interact with the garbage collector, except through brute force methods such as `System.gc`.

The `java.lang.ref` package was introduced as part of Java 2. Figure A-4 shows the class hierarchy for the classes in this package. This package defines reference-object classes that enable a limited degree of interaction with the garbage collector. `Reference` objects are used to maintain a reference to some other object in such a way that the collector can still reclaim the target object. As you might expect, the addition of these new reference objects complicates the concept of reachability as defined in the object lifecycle. Understanding this is important,

Resurrection

It is possible to create new strong references to an object while executing the `finalizer` method. This puts the object back into an in-use state. This practice, known as *resurrection*, is a bad idea. The specification guarantees that a finalizer is run at most one time per object. Because the finalizer is not run a second time, resurrecting an object can lead to serious problems.

For more information about resurrection, see Ken Arnold and James Gosling, *The Java Programming Language*, Section 2.10.2. Addison-Wesley, 1998.

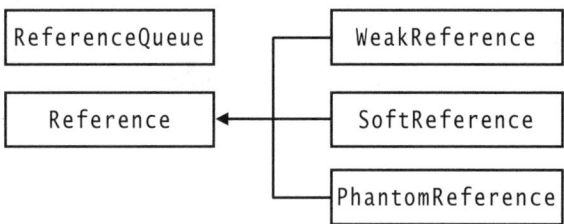

Figure A-4   Reference class hierarchy

even if you don't intend to make direct use of this package. Some of the core class libraries use `WeakReferences` internally, so you might encounter them while using memory profilers to track memory usage.

A.4.1   Types of Reference Objects

Three types of reference objects are provided, each weaker than the last: soft, weak, and phantom. Each type corresponds to a different level of reachability:

- Soft references are for implementing memory-sensitive caches.

- Weak references are for implementing mappings that do not prevent their keys (or values) from being reclaimed.

- Phantom references are for scheduling pre-mortem cleanup actions in a more flexible way than is possible with the Java finalization mechanism.

Going from strongest to weakest, the different levels of reachability reflect the lifecycle of an object:

- An object is strongly reachable if some thread can reach it without traversing any reference objects.

- An object is softly reachable if it is not strongly reachable but can be reached by traversing a soft reference.

- An object is weakly reachable if it is neither strongly nor softly reachable but can be reached by traversing a weak reference. When the weak references to a weakly reachable object are cleared, the object becomes eligible for finalization.

- An object is phantom reachable if it is neither strongly, softly, nor weakly reachable, it has been finalized, and some phantom reference refers to it.

- An object is unreachable, and therefore eligible for reclamation, when it is not reachable in any of the preceding ways.

A.4.2   Example GC with `WeakReference`

You're likely to encounter special reference objects while using tools to look for memory leaks. Only strong references will directly interfere with garbage collection. If you find chains of objects linked by weak references, you should be able to ignore them from a GC perspective. (For additional information on the use of special reference objects, see the API documentation.)

Figure A-5 shows a graph of objects in memory for a sample program. Let's say that the problem with this program is that the `Dog` objects are not being collected, leading to a memory leak. By using a memory profiler, you can find all the pointers to the `Dog` object and follow them back to their GC roots. There are two GC roots in Figure A-5, a static variable in class `Kennel` and a stack frame in a live thread. In this case, the `WagTask` thread is in an infinite loop, forcing the dog's tail to wag. The question is how to get rid of the `Dog` object.

There are two references pointing to the `Dog` object, but only one of them is interesting from a GC perspective. The `WeakReference` from the `dogCache` is not important. The interesting reference is the reference from the `Tail`, which chains from a stack frame in a live thread. To free the `Dog`, and the associated `Tail`, you need to terminate the thread that is wagging the `Tail`. Once this thread is gone, everything falls into place. When an object that is pointed to by a `WeakReference` is collected, the `WeakReference` is automatically set to `null`. Figure A-6 shows the result of terminating the wag thread.

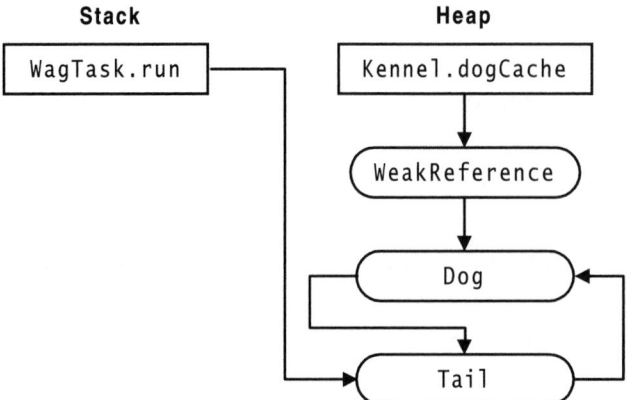

Figure A-5   Reference graph

When the thread dies, its stack is removed. Now the only strong reference to the Dog is via the Tail, and this becomes a simple circular reference that isn't reachable from a GC root. The Dog, and by extension the Tail, are no longer strongly reachable through any references. They are only weakly reachable through the dogCache. When the collector discovers this (which it does on its own schedule), it might set the weak reference to null, making the Dog and Tail totally unreachable. They then become candidates for collection and will be removed at the collector's discretion.

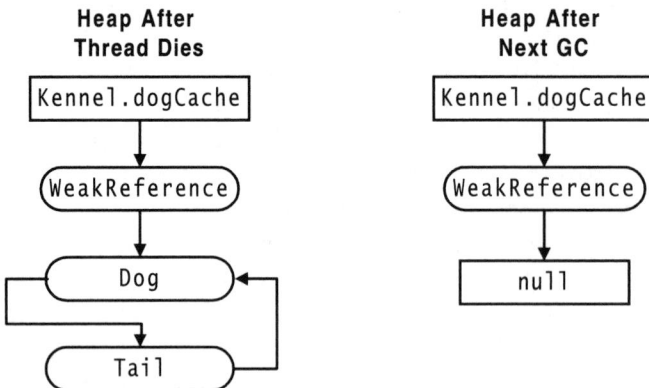

Figure A-6   Results of garbage collection

A.5   References on Garbage Collection

Arnold, Ken, and James Gosling. *The Java Programming Language, Second Edition*, Addison-Wesley, Reading, MA, 1998.

Gosling, James, Bill Joy, and Guy Steele. *The Java Language Specification, Second Edition*, Addison-Wesley, Reading, MA, 2000.

Jones, Richard, and Rafael Lins. *Garbage Collection: Algorithms for Automatic Dynamic Memory Management*, John Wiley & Sons, New York, 1996.

Lindholm, Tim and Frank Yellin. *The Java Virtual Machine Specification, Second Edition*, Addison-Wesley, Reading, MA, 1999.

The Java HotSpot
Virtual Machine

THE *Java Virtual Machine Specification*[1] describes the various behaviors that a JVM implementation must perform. However, there are many ways to implement these behaviors. Sun's original version of the JVM, which evolved from version 1.0 through version 1.2.2, was based on technology that had been in use for many years in other systems. Then, in 1999, Sun released the first version of the Java HotSpot virtual machine. The HotSpot VM uses cutting-edge techniques in the areas of memory management, thread synchronization, and dynamic compilation.

While most of the material in this book is relevant no matter which JVM you use, the HotSpot VM does represent an important part of the Java Platform's performance landscape. Starting with the J2SE v. 1.3 SDK, all of Sun's JVM implementations will be based on HotSpot technology. Also, several other vendors have licensed the HotSpot code base for inclusion in their own implementation of the JRE.

This appendix provides an overview of the HotSpot architecture and discusses how the HotSpot VM achieves improved performance. Sections B.4 and B.5 summarize the various option settings that can be used to control the behavior of the HotSpot VM at runtime.

B.1   HotSpot Architecture

There are two main parts to the HotSpot system: the runtime and the compiler (Figure B-1). The runtime portion includes a bytecode interpreter, memory management and garbage collection functionality, and machinery for handling thread synchronization and other low-level tasks. The compiler's job is simply to translate bytecodes into native machine instructions, thus improving execution speed.

---

1. Tim Lindholm and Frank Yellin, *The Java Virtual Machine Specification, Second Edition*, Section 3.5.3. Addison-Wesley, 1999.

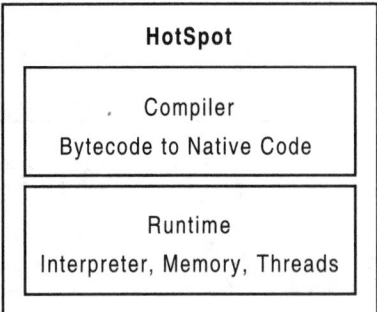

Figure B-1   HotSpot architecture

Note that it is possible to use the HotSpot VM as a fully compliant JVM without the compiler. The only difference will be a decrease in performance.

B.1.1   Two Versions of HotSpot

When the first version of the HotSpot VM was shipped in April 1999, it was dubbed the Java HotSpot Performance Engine. The Java HotSpot Performance Engine made major improvements in the performance of many server-side applications. However, it wasn't ideal for many client-side programs. The requirements for client and server can be quite different. For example, client programs often favor lower RAM footprint and faster start-up time over maximum computational performance. Due to these different requirements, the HotSpot technology was split into two lines—one for the client and one for the server. Figure B-2 shows how this breaks down.

> ## HotSpot Compiler != `javac`
>
> The terminology used here can be confusing. The `javac` tool included with the J2SDK is a source-code to bytecode compiler. The "compiler" included with the HotSpot VM is a bytecode to native machine-code compiler. Though they're both generically referred to as compilers, they perform very different tasks. This terminology sometimes leads to the mistaken impression that you have to compile your source code with a different compiler to use the HotSpot VM. This is not the case. Any class files that execute on older JVMs should run under the HotSpot VM without modification.

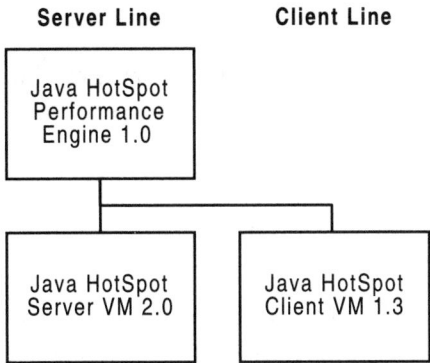

Figure B-2   HotSpot product lines

As of version 1.3 of the J2SE SDK, all of Sun's implementations include a version of the HotSpot Client VM. The HotSpot Server VM is an optional add-on. The Client VM and the Server VM are very similar, and actually share a lot of code. The only part of the system that is different is the compiler. The Server VM contains a highly advanced adaptive compiler that supports many of the same types of optimizations performed by optimizing C++ compilers (as well as a few optimizations C++ compilers only wish they could do). The Client VM is much simpler. It doesn't try to perform many of the more complex optimizations performed by the compiler in the Server VM, but in exchange the Client VM requires less time to analyze and compile a particular piece of code. This means that the Client VM can start up faster, and requires less warm-up time to reach peak performance. Figure B-3 shows the two systems—only the shaded areas are significantly different.

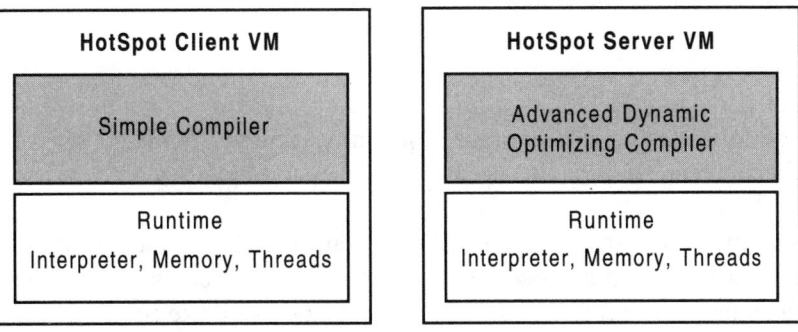

Figure B-3   HotSpot Client and HotSpot Server

B.2   Runtime Features

Both the HotSpot Client VM and the HotSpot Server VM share the same runtime code. The runtime is primarily responsible for the following types of operations:

* Interpretation of bytecodes
* Memory allocation and garbage collection
* Thread synchronization

Simple JIT compilers compile all methods before they are executed. This turns out to be wasteful, as many methods are only executed once (or a very few times). In such cases, the time to compile the method can dwarf the time required to execute it. All this compilation also increases memory usage because the compiled code must be stored. As a result, the HotSpot runtime executes many methods in a purely interpreted mode. To ensure maximum performance for these methods, the HotSpot runtime provides a highly optimized bytecode interpreter.

In addition to the bytecode interpreter, the runtime is responsible for memory management and thread synchronization. The HotSpot runtime provides several important optimizations in these areas.

B.2.1   Memory Allocation and Garbage Collection

As previously discussed, how you handle memory is of critical importance to the performance of your software. While there are many optimizations that can reduce memory requirements, you will always need to allocate and collect objects. One of the HotSpot VM's most important features is its superior memory allocator and garbage collector. The HotSpot runtime provides an exact, generational, incremental, state-of-the-art garbage collector. (Chapter 7, Object Mutability: Strings and Other Things, also contains information on this subject.)

Accuracy

The HotSpot garbage collector is a *fully accurate* collector. In contrast, many other garbage collectors are conservative or partially accurate. While conservative garbage collection can be attractive because it is easy to implement, it has certain drawbacks.

A conservative collector does not know for sure where all object references are located. As a result, it must assume that memory words that appear to refer to an object are in fact object references. This means that it can make certain kinds of mistakes, such as confusing an integer for an object pointer. This has several negative impacts.

First, when such mistakes are made (which in practice is not very often), memory leaks can occur unpredictably in ways that are virtually impossible for application programmers to reproduce or debug (although crashes caused by dangling object references are still prevented, and the program still executes correctly if there is enough spare memory).

Second, since it might have made a mistake, a conservative collector must either use handles to refer indirectly to objects (decreasing performance), or avoid relocating objects. Relocating handleless objects requires that all of the references to the object be updated, which cannot be done if the collector does not know for sure that an apparent reference is a real reference. The inability to relocate objects causes object memory fragmentation and, more importantly, prevents use of the advanced generational copying collection algorithms described below.

Because the HotSpot collector is fully accurate, it can make several strong design guarantees that a conservative collector cannot make:

* All logically inaccessible object memory can be reclaimed reliably.

* All objects can be relocated, allowing object memory compaction to eliminate object memory fragmentation and increases memory locality.

Generational Copying Collection

The HotSpot runtime employs a state-of-the-art generational copying collector[2] that provides two major benefits:

* Major increases in both allocation speed and overall garbage collection efficiency (often by more than a factor of 5) for most programs, compared to the Java 2 SDK

* A corresponding decrease in the frequency of user-perceivable garbage collection pauses

A generational collector takes advantage of the fact that, in most programs, the vast majority of objects (often greater than 95 percent) are very short-lived. (In other words, they're used as temporary data structures.) By allocating objects from a dedicated object "nursery," a generational collector can accomplish several things. First, because new objects are allocated contiguously in stacklike fashion in the object nursery, allocation becomes extremely fast. This is because it involves merely updating a single pointer and performing a single check for nursery overflow. Second, by the time the nursery overflows, most of the objects in the nursery are already "dead," allowing the garbage collector to simply move the few

---

2. For more information about generational copying collectors, see Richard Jones and Rafael Lins, *Garbage Collection: Algorithms for Automatic Dynamic Memory Management*, pp. 143–180. John Wiley & Sons, 1996.

surviving objects elsewhere. This way, it avoids doing any reclamation work for dead objects in the nursery.

Mark-Compact "Old Object" Collector

Although the generational copying collector collects most dead objects efficiently, longer-lived objects still accumulate in the "old object" memory area (old objects are objects that have existed for a while in machine terms). Occasionally, based on low-memory conditions or programmatic requests, an old-object garbage collection must be performed. The HotSpot runtime can use a standard mark-compact[3] collection algorithm, which traverses the entire graph of live objects from its "roots," and then sweeps through memory, compacting away the gaps left by dead objects. By compacting gaps in the heap rather than collecting them into a free list, memory fragmentation is eliminated, and old-object allocation is streamlined by eliminating freelist searching.

Incremental "Pauseless" Garbage Collector

The mark-compact collector does not eliminate all user-perceivable pauses. User-perceived GC pauses occur when old objects need to be garbage collected, and these pauses are proportional to the amount of live object data that exists. This means that the pauses can become arbitrarily large as more data is manipulated, which is a very undesirable property for server applications, animations, and other soft real-time applications.

The HotSpot runtime provides an alternative old-space garbage collector to solve this problem. This collector is fully incremental,[4] eliminating most user-detectable garbage collection pauses. This incremental collector scales smoothly, providing relatively constant pause times even when extremely large object datasets are being manipulated. This provides excellent behavior for:

- Server applications, especially high-availability applications
- Applications that manipulate very large live object data sets
- Applications where all user-noticeable pauses are undesirable, such as games, animations, and other highly interactive applications

The pauseless collector works by using an incremental old-space collection scheme referred to academically as the "train" algorithm. This algorithm breaks up old-space collection pauses into many tiny pauses (typically less than 10 milliseconds) that can be spread out over time so that the program virtually never

---

3. For more information about the mark-compact collection algorithm, see Jones and Lins, pp. 97–114.
4. For more information about incremental collectors, see Jones and Lins, pp. 183–223.

appears to pause to a user. Since the train algorithm is not a hard real-time algorithm, it cannot guarantee an upper limit on pause times; however, in practice much larger pauses are extremely rare, and are not caused directly by large datasets.

The pauseless collector also has the highly desirable side benefit of producing improved memory locality. This happens because the algorithm works by attempting to relocate groups of tightly coupled objects into regions of adjacent memory, which provides excellent paging and cache locality properties for those objects. This can also benefit highly multithreaded applications that operate on distinct sets of object data.

B.2.2   Thread Synchronization

Another big attraction of the Java programming language is the provision of language-level thread synchronization, which makes it easy to write multithreaded programs with fine-grained locking. Unfortunately, older JVMs' synchronization implementations are highly inefficient relative to other micro-operations in the Java programming language, making use of fine-grain synchronization a major performance bottleneck.

HotSpot incorporates a unique synchronization implementation that boosts performance substantially. The synchronization mechanism provides its performance benefits by providing ultra-fast, constant-time performance for all uncontended synchronizations, which dynamically comprise the great majority of synchronizations.

The Java HotSpot synchronization implementation is fully suitable for multiprocessing, and exhibits excellent multiprocessor performance characteristics.

B.3   HotSpot Server Compiler

While the HotSpot Client VM uses fairly traditional compilation technology, the HotSpot Server VM uses many advanced techniques to achieve maximum computational performance. A few of these optimizations are described in the next three sections.

B.3.1   Aggressive Inlining

Method inlining is an important compiler optimization. However, static compilers are restricted in the amount of inlining they can do, for a couple of reasons. First, a static compiler can inline a method only if the compiler can determine that method is not overridden in a subclass. A static compiler can inline `static`, `final`, and `private` methods because it knows those methods can't be overridden. However, `public` and `protected` methods can be overridden in a subclass, and static compilers therefore cannot inline those methods.

Second, even if it were possible to determine through static analysis which methods are overridden and which are not, a static compiler still could not inline `public` and `protected` methods. The Java language allows classes to be loaded during runtime, and such dynamically loaded classes can change the structure of a program significantly. In particular, such dynamic loading can render invalid any inlining that was done based on pre-runtime, static analyses.

The HotSpot dynamic compiler uses runtime analysis to perform inlining aggressively, yet safely. Once the HotSpot profiler has collected runtime information about program hot spots, it not only compiles the hot spot into native code, but also performs extensive method inlining on that code. The HotSpot compiler can afford to be aggressive in the way it inlines because it can always back out an inlining optimization if it determines that the method inheritance structure has changed during runtime due to dynamic class loading.

The HotSpot VM can revert to using the interpreter whenever compiler deoptimizations are called for because of dynamic class loading. When a class is loaded dynamically, the HotSpot VM checks to ensure that the interclass dependencies of inlined methods have not been altered. If a dynamically loaded class affects any dependencies, the HotSpot VM can back out affected inlined code, revert to interpreting for a while, and reoptimize later based on the new class dependencies.

On the other hand, when running statically compiled code, a JVM does not have access to the original bytecodes, and cannot fall back on an interpreter when optimizations in the statically compiled code become unsafe. Therefore, static compilers cannot be as aggressive in their optimizations as dynamic compilers, which results in slower performance.

The extensive inlining enabled by the dynamic compiler gives it a huge advantage over static compilers. Inlining reduces the number of method invocations and their associated performance overhead. This is a significant bonus with the Java programming language, in which methods are virtual by default and method invocations are frequent.

Method inlining is also synergistic with other optimizations. Inlining produces large blocks of code that make additional optimizations easier for the compiler to perform. The HotSpot Server compiler's ability to perform aggressive inlining is a key factor in making it faster than current JIT and static compilers.

B.3.2   Other Optimizations

The optimizer performs all of the classic optimizations such as dead code elimination, loop invariant hoisting, common subexpression elimination, and constant propagation. It also features optimizations more specific to Java technology, such as null-check elimination. The register allocator is a global graph coloring allocator and makes full use of large register sets.

B.3.3   Array Bounds Checks

None of the current generation of HotSpot compilers eliminate unnecessary array bounds checks. While it is theoretically possible to automatically remove many array bounds-related computations from certain types of loop structures, the HotSpot compiler doesn't yet do this. The HotSpot engineering team has run tests that show that only a small improvement in performance on the SpecJVM benchmark is to be expected when this feature is implemented. Specific applications might see much larger increases, however, depending on the amount of array access that they perform.

B.4   -X Flags

Both the HotSpot Client and Server VMs enable some control over the performance of the virtual machine. In some special circumstances, these options can be important. *Keep in mind, however, that they are all nonstandard and subject to change without notice.* Table B-1 shows all of the special HotSpot options.

Option	Description
`-Xmixed`	Mixed mode execution (default)
`-Xint`	Interpreted mode execution only
`-Xbootclasspath:<directories and zip/jar files separated by ;>`	Set search path for bootstrap classes and resources
`-Xnoclassgc`	Disable class garbage collection
`-Xincgc`	Enable incremental garbage collection
`-Xbatch`	Disable background compilation

Table B-1   HotSpot Options

Option	Description
`-Xms<size>`	Set initial Java heap size
`-Xmx<size>`	Set maximum Java heap size
`-Xprof`	Output CPU profiling data

Table B-1   HotSpot Options

B.4.1 -Xnoclassgc

This flag turns off class unloading. Under JDK 1.1.x, this was important in some circumstances. With Java 2, however, the semantics of class loading are such that you really don't ever need to use this flag.

B.4.2 -Xincgc

This option enables the incremental garbage collector and reduces the average length of garbage collection pauses. Even without the incremental collector, pauses are usually not user-detectable. However, some applications have stringent requirements about how often certain operations need to happen. The incremental collector isn't designed for hard real-time applications, but can be useful in many soft real-time situations where concrete guarantees about CPU time are not required.

B.4.3 -Xbatch

This flag disables background compilation. By default, the HotSpot VM can compile methods in the background while they are executing. This smooths operation by eliminating the pauses that can occur when waiting for a method to be compiled. However, compiling methods in the background does have a slight performance impact. Using the -Xbatch flag on server processes that don't directly interact with the user might result in higher peak performance on single-processor servers. In general, using this flag hurts performance on multiprocessor machines because compilation could otherwise be off-loaded to a different processor.

B.4.4 -Xms

This flag sets the initial size of the object heap. The current default is 2MB. Increasing this size can help improve startup time for applications that need large heaps by eliminating the extra garbage collection that occurs before the heap is automatically expanded.

B.4.5   -Xmx

This flag sets the maximum size of the Java heap. It currently defaults to 64MB. If the program needs to allocate more memory than is allowed by the current setting of the max heap size, then the system will throw an OutOfMemoryError. Programs that work on very large amounts of data might need to increase this value.

B.4.6   -Xprof

The HotSpot VM includes a fairly simple CPU profiling tool. While it isn't a replacement for a full-featured commercial tool, it is quick and easy to use. It also gives some useful information about HotSpot internals that can be interesting.

To use this profiler, simply include the -Xprof option on the command line when you start your program. The profiler option gives you a basic CPU profiler. It does not provide any memory profiling options. When a thread terminates, a report, such as the one shown in Figure B-4, is printed to the console.

This profiler shows the methods that used the most time during that thread's lifetime. The methods are divided into three categories:

- Interpreted
- Compiled
- Stub

Interpreted methods are executed by the bytecode interpreter. As shown in Figure B-4, almost 10 percent of the program's time was spent in methods run by the interpreter. However, this is deceptive. You'll notice that there are two columns. The Native column shows the amount of time spent in native C methods called by interpreted methods. Thus, when you break it down that way, this program spends very little time in the interpreter, only a few ticks.

Compiled methods are those that are translated from bytecode to machine code by the compiler. In this case, that is where the program is spending most of its time. Note that it is possible for compiled methods to call out to native C functions, although that doesn't show up in this profile.

The Stub category shows methods called though JNI. The Stub column shows the amount of time it took to set up the call, while the Native column shows the amount of time spent in the native function.

```
Interpreted + native Method
3.7% 0 + 8 java.io.FileInputStream.readBytes
1.9% 0 + 4 java.io.FileOutputStream.open
0.9% 0 + 2 java.io.FileOutputStream.writeBytes
0.9% 0 + 2 java.io.FileInputStream.open
0.5% 0 + 1 java.io.FileInputStream.read
0.5% 0 + 1 FastCopyFile.copy
0.5% 0 + 1 java.io.Win32FileSystem.canonicalize
0.5% 1 + 0 java.io.BufferedReader.readLine
0.5% 0 + 1 java.io.BufferedInputStream.<init>
9.7% 1 + 20 Total interpreted

Compiled + native Method
30.6% 66 + 0 java.io.BufferedInputStream.read
29.6% 64 + 0 java.io.BufferedOutputStream.write
8.8% 19 + 0 FastCopyFile.copy
4.6% 10 + 0 java.io.BufferedInputStream.ensureOpen
0.5% 1 + 0 java.io.BufferedReader.readLine
74.1% 160 + 0 Total compiled

Stub + native Method
9.7% 0 + 21 java.io.FileOutputStream.writeBytes
3.2% 0 + 7 java.io.FileInputStream.readBytes
13.0% 0 + 28 Total stub

Thread-local ticks:
2.8% 6 Class loader
0.5% 1 Unknown code

Global summary of 2.89 seconds:
100.0% 222 Received ticks
1.4% 3 Threads_lock blocks
97.3% 216 Delivered ticks
97.3% 216 All ticks
2.7% 6 Class loader
0.5% 1 Unknown code
```

Figure B-4   HotSpot profiler results

The Global Summary at the end of the profile provides useful information such as how much time the thread spent blocked, and how much time was spent loading classes.

B.5   -XX Flags

While the flags in Section B.4 are subject to change at any time, the flags in this section are even less reliable. The flags described in this section are for experimentation purposes only. *They aren't documented as part of the HotSpot release, and are not supported in any way.* Use them at your own risk!

B.5.1   Kinds of -XX Flags

There are really two kinds of -XX flags. The first is a Boolean flag. The second is an Integer flag. Boolean flags are used in the following manner:

    -XX:<+/-><flagname>

For example, passing the following string as an option to the `java` command would activate the `GoFaster` option if one existed.

    -XX:+GoFaster

To turn this option off (if it was on by default) you would pass

    -XX:-GoFaster

Integer flags are a little different. For example, the following string would set the `NumCylinders` option to eight.

    -XX:NumCylinders=8

The next few paragraphs describe some of the more interesting flags.

B.5.2 `PrintBytecodeHistogram`

Default Value: `false`
Example Usage: `java -XX:+PrintBytecodeHistogram <yourclass>`

This option prints out statistics that show what bytecodes were executed while your program was running. Some sample output from this option is shown in Figure B-5. This type of information isn't commonly used when performance tuning typical programs, but might be of interest to researchers.

B.5.3 `CompileThreshold`

Default Value: 1500
Example Usage: `java -XX:CompileThreshold=1000000 <yourclass>`

The current implementation of HotSpot usually waits for a method to be executed a certain number of times before it is compiled. Not compiling every method helps startup time and reduces RAM footprint. This option allows you to control that threshold. By increasing the number, you can trade slight reductions in RAM footprint in exchange for a longer period of time before your program reaches peak performance.

```
Histogram of 324363 executed bytecodes:
 absolute relative code name
 -----------------------------
33403 10.30% 15 iload
14378 4.43% 84 iinc
13578 4.19% 19 aload
12234 3.77% d2 fast_aload_0
12095 3.73% a1 if_icmplt
12057 3.72% 1b iload_1
11234 3.46% 1c iload_2
[lots of stuff snipped out here]
45 0.01% 06 iconst_3
43 0.01% 20 lload_2
42 0.01% d0 fast_lldc_w
34 0.01% 86 i2f
34 0.01% 6a fmul
34 0.01% 8b f2i
 -----------------------------
323938 99.87% (cutoff = 0.01%)    0 .
```

Figure B-5   Bytecode histogram

B.5.4 NewSize

Default Value: 655360
Example Usage: java -XX:NewSize=196608 <yourclass>

This option allows you to control the default size of the New generation (also known as the nursery) of the HotSpot VM's generational garbage collector. Increasing the amount of new space means that fewer objects will have to be copied to old space. However, a small new space can be scavenged more quickly, and works better with processor caches.

References

Abrash, Michael. *Graphics Programming Black Book, Special Edition*, The Coriolis Group, Scottsdale, AZ, 1997. ISBN 1576101746.

Arnold, Ken, and James Gosling. *The Java Programming Language, Second Edition*, Addison-Wesley, Reading, MA, 1998. ISBN 0201310066.

Binstock, Andrew, and John Rex. *Practical Algorithms for Programmers*, Addison-Wesley, Reading, MA, 1995. ISBN 020163208X.

Booch, Grady. *Object-Oriented Analysis and Design with Applications, Second Edition*, Addison-Wesley, Reading, MA, 1994. ISBN 0805353402.

Campione, Mary, and Kathy Walrath. *The Java Tutorial, Second Edition: Object-Oriented Programming for the Internet*, Addison-Wesley, Reading, MA, 1998. ISBN 0201310074.

Gamma, Erich, Richard Helm, Ralph Johnson, and John Vlissides. *Design Patterns: Elements of Reusable Object-Oriented Software*, Addison-Wesley, Reading, MA, 1995. ISBN 0201633612.

Goldstein, Neal, and Jeff Alger. *Developing Object-Oriented Software for the Macintosh: Analysis, Design, and Programming*, Addison-Wesley, Reading, MA, 1992. ISBN 0201570653.

Gosling, James, Bill Joy, and Guy Steele. *The Java Language Specification, Second Edition*, Addison-Wesley, Reading, MA, 2000.

Grand, Mark. *Patterns in Java, Volume 1*, John Wiley & Sons, New York, 1998. ISBN 0471258393.

Jones, Richard, and Rafael Lins. *Garbage Collection: Algorithms for Automatic Dynamic Memory Management*, John Wiley & Sons, New York, 1996. ISBN 0471941484.

Larman, Craig. *Applying UML and Patterns: An Introduction to Object-Oriented Analysis and Design*, Prentice Hall, Upper Saddle River, NJ, 1998. ISBN 0137488807.

Lea, Doug. *Concurrent Programming in Java: Design Principles and Patterns, Second Edition*, Addison-Wesley, Reading, MA, 1999. ISBN 0201310090.

Liang, Sheng. *The Java Native Interface: Programmer's Guide and Specification*, Addison-Wesley, Reading, MA, 1999. ISBN 0201325772.

Lindholm, Tim, and Frank Yellin. *The Java Virtual Machine Specification, Second Edition,* Addison-Wesley, Reading, MA, 1999. ISBN 0201432943.

Schneider, Geri, and Jason Winters. *Applying Use Cases: A Practical Guide*, Addison-Wesley, Reading, MA, 1998. ISBN 0201309815.

Sedgewick, Robert. *Algorithms, Second Edition*, Addison-Wesley, Reading, MA, 1988. ISBN 0201066726.

Index

The Java™ Series

ISBN 0-201-70433-1

ISBN 0-201-70323-8

ISBN 0-201-70393-9

ISBN 0-201-48558-3

ISBN 0-201-43299-4

ISBN 0-201-43297-8

ISBN 0-201-31002-3

ISBN 0-201-31003-1

ISBN 0-201-48552-4

ISBN 0-201-70329-7

ISBN 0-201-31000-7

ISBN 0-201-31008-2

ISBN 0-201-63453-8

ISBN 0-201-63459-7

ISBN 0-201-63456-2

ISBN 0-201-70277-0

ISBN 0-201-31009-0

ISBN 0-201-70502-8

ISBN 0-201-32577-2

ISBN 0-201-43294-3

ISBN 0-201-70456-0

ISBN 0-201-71041-2

ISBN 0-201-43321-4

ISBN 0-201-43328-1

ISBN 0-201-70969-4

Please see our web site (http://www.awl.com/cseng/javaseries)
for more information on these titles.